A
Philosophical
History of
Love

A
Philosophical
History of
Love

Wayne
Cristaudo

Transaction Publishers
New Brunswick (U.S.A.) and London (U.K.)

Library of Congress Catalog Number: 2011044826
ISBN: 978-1-4128-4626-4
Printed in the United States of America

Library of Congress Cataloging-in-Publication Data

Cristaudo, Wayne, 1954-
    A philosophical history of love / Wayne Cristaudo.
       p. cm.
    Includes bibliographical references and index.
    ISBN 978-1-4128-4626-4
    1. Love—Western countries—History. I. Title.
    BD436.C73 2012
    128'.4609—dc23

                                                          2011044826

I could not believe in the Holy Ghost unless He had changed His form of expression relentlessly.

—Eugen Rosenstock-Huessy, *The Fruit of Lips,* 33

Contents

Preface

This book is based upon the premise that love and evil are substances (in the sense of substance used by Aristotle, that they are real existents) and are subjects of spirit—indeed, they are spirits.[1] But this is not to accept the strict dualism of spirit and matter—a spirit of a friendship is no less real than the people who are friends, a spirit both mirrors and infuses relationships. It expresses and reconfigures relationships. Furthermore, a spirit either nourishes or depletes members of a group. Thus, how could it not be real? The naturalistic dogmas about reality are no less an obstacle to how we experience reality than the idealist ones. Unfortunately, naturalism is embedded in the entire method and vocabulary of modern analytic philosophy. To see this, one need only compare Descartes's reductionist rules for a method with analytical philosophy's reductionist approach to language.

So much of the lovelessness of the modern world stems from a dogmatic, ostensibly "scientific" decision to drive love out of the cosmos, and only let it reenter through the template that is designed for predictability and causal connections. Thus, a way of looking at life which, in spite of various cultural and historical antithetical nuances and emphases, was steeped in metaphor, analogy, and parable was relegated to "entertainment." Concomitantly, an approach to reality that was derived from that part of our nature which is contrary to the silent mechanisms and forces which precede speech and which comes from our primordial speaking nature and need to express and narrate, to move each other with fear and love was relegated to the unreal. And now we are supposed to understand how to manage and rule reality—we are ostensibly, as Descartes, one of the earliest advocates and metaphysical builders of the world we now inhabit, put it, "lords and masters of nature." Though, is it not conspicuous how little contentment there is in this sovereignty, and how desperate (and often foolish) are our romantic reactions to the desert of our sovereignty?

In our cause and effect understanding of reality, men and women all too easily forget their role in their world, their relationships to life. What Michel Foucault called discursive regimes conspire today at levels of education, philosophy, commerce, management, and economics to push a worldview which not only makes the world more loveless, but which denies that love is a serious power of any consequence. These discursive regimes would make us all prisoners of their own epistemologies and methods, hence of their knowledge, but what they never realize is that that also means that we become subjects of their ignorance. Of course, those who live of these regimes believe, indeed insist that they have the methods and the knowledge that will make us free. If Descartes commences modernity with universal doubt, the new mandarins continue it without a shadow of doubt in their own ability to be the lords and masters and judges over our perceptions of reality. The authorities of these "discursive regimes" are oblivious to an important truth, viz. that love (and this is also true of evil) provides the incalculable founding of an event, the source of a new attractor field, which reconfigures our knowledge and the various discursive regimes which constitute social knowledge and power. Had they read some Schelling they may have known this, but then their self-certainty and aspirations for social dominance would be severely curbed, which would not fit their own will to power.

This book rests on the premise that love itself is a subject and that it is striving to realize itself. It tells the historical story of some of those spirits which love has sent forth and which have historically shaped the institutions and values of the Western world. Those spirits have not always been for the good—for what is deficient in what is loved shapes the very spirit of that love. Thus, the emphasis upon knowledge and virtue by the moderns—that we still hunger for more nourishing spirits of love. But each of the spirits of love that have "evolved" has done so in response to some crisis or other. Our bad loves put us in hell; the greatness of great love is that it opens up exits hitherto unimaginable.

As heirs to the Jewish and Christian understandings of the sacred (albeit intermingled with various other "idolatrous" renditions of desire), modern Western men and women have a sense of love's measure, of the kinds and scales of love's loves. I would be dishonest were I not to state from the outset that I think that Jewish and, in spite of all their differences, Christian understandings of the sacred say something fundamentally true about reality, and love's role within it. Christianity may usurp and distort the Jewish traditions of its origin, but, in spite of the inimical nature and rivalry of these tradition, Christianity cannot shake off its Jewish heritage—and Jewish people are also as much caught up in the logic of institutions that evolved out of Europe and hence Christian nations as Christians are. Indeed to the extent that all European peoples are, in spite of their conscious beliefs and stances toward religion, Christianized and thus even, to a not insignificant extent Judaized, I find it foolish to dispense with religious names and language which are constitutive of the history of the West. Insofar as I argue that the experience and a certain emphasis upon aspects of love is the basis of the religions of Judaism and Christianity, I stand in danger of alienating traditionally religious people who want their God to be more than love creating and redeeming itself and its own creations, as well as the atheists who will have little time for a vocabulary steeped in religion. From Rosenstock-Huessy and Franz Rosenzweig (though Spinoza and Locke also knew this, which was why in their dreams of modernizing they wanted to reclassify all of reality with new names tested against experience), I have learnt that the powers of the world cannot be divorced from the names which we deploy to call each other into action. Thus, I am totally perplexed when a historian like Norman Davies writes a mighty tome on Europe and devotes such a tiny proportion to Christianity. For it is completely irrelevant whether one is or not a Christian or Jew today to appreciate that for most of its history the European world was constituted by institutions, liturgies, rituals, literature, wars and revolutions, celebrations, festivities, and holidays whose very names indicated what forces people believed they were responding to. And those forces and the semantic field in which they flourished were inseparable from the faith of the living whose lives were ruled by those forces they summoned and sealed with religious names. In the nineteenth century the German philosopher, who left such a big impression, at least for a short time, on Karl Marx, Ludwig Feuerbach attempted to demonstrate that Humanity is the subject and God the object, but humans have taken alienated humanity (i.e., God) as the creator. I am deeply sympathetic with Feuerbach, and his later emphasis upon the role of dialogue and love in communities is something I strongly concur with (he speaks of I and thou long before Martin Buber). But Feuerbach makes one big error, and it is a similar error to Marx and Nietzsche and indeed it is the error pertaining to what the great Jewish philosopher Franz Rosenzweig called "the anthropological turn": it is the error of placing too much weight upon consciousness and too little upon life itself. The twentieth century has paid dearly for the *hubris* of those who thought we could plan and create pretty much any order we like. The fact is, we do not know ourselves very well, and we do not know what tomorrow brings; moreover, we never will. For my part, I think it is undeniable that human beings are ever confronted with gaps and radiances. (Leonard Cohen in his wonderful song "Anthem" spoke of the cracks in everything being where the light gets in.) God is a traditional name for that which radiates through the gaps of the self. I am less interested whether that name is retained, and whether the encounter is best prepared through liturgy and ritual than I am in trying to play a part in enabling people to see the danger of thinking they are self-consciously sufficient and that we can exist in closed totalities of reason. As creative, sustaining, and redeeming love and its misdirection (evil) and total lack (hate) are absolutely intrinsic to how we and tomorrow are formed, I am content to take the love that is both the central attribute of the power traditionally named as God as well as the power that most people, irrespective of their preferred vocabulary, find of the highest existential significance as the subject of the radiance. But rather than dispensing with the names of the religious tradition I wish to use them—not because I want people to believe in anything or anyone but because I wish to attune people to domains and dimensions of experience which were once intrinsic to those signs. Put more bluntly, throughout where I use religious terminology my purpose is historical, sociological, and anthropological—and what is truly intrinsic to our existence cannot but be historical, sociological and anthropological. This is why at times, in this work, it may seem to the reader as if I have simply moved from discussing love to discussing theology. But that is not the case. Love is ever the subject here—the theological excavations are undertaken to dig out more about love by digging deeper into the meaning of the sign of what so many and for so long have taken as love's greatest significance.

Whether or not the symbols expressing that truth can still be understood by the majority of people whose mental maps have been shaped by certain dogmas of the mechanistic revolution is debatable—which may well tell us more about a modern deficiency to appreciate the most potent symbols of spirit than about the truth conveyed by the symbols themselves. And that is why I am loathe to believe that modern thinkers are better thinkers about life, in general, and love's role within it than premoderns. In any case, this much we know: that we moderns have learnt many of love's lessons over time, that some of its most important aspects, its spirits, were released at particular times as responses to particular crises and catastrophes. But what begins as love quickly becomes its opposite, which is why our institutions must evolve to keep pace with love's transformative demands—and where they fail to keep pace, they become dungeons. And because we are mimetic creatures—which is what modern notions of freedom and authenticity invariably forget—where love goes awry it inevitably becomes a social evil, and eventually a social catastrophe, a mass scaffold, and mass grave.

I think the tragedy of Western men and women is that they seek love but always and ever love an aspect of it, i.e. love it through its distortions, and thus lose the very end they pursue. This work pursues a history of love's evolution in the West (and my decision to limit myself to the West is because I have studied the West my entire adult life and simply do not have the knowledge to do a global analysis), it does so, though, in order to enable us to see what is still left and why its various spirits are important for us.

Through this work I occasionally also engage with René Girard. I am no disciple of Girard and, at times, find him infuriatingly one dimensional, and in spite of his preoccupation with violence, I find he neglects too much of the viscera of our nature by implying that mimesis itself is the major component of desire's nature. I do not agree with that, but Girard is right to draw our attention to the frequent rivalry of lovers, the envy that creates scarcity where it need not be (nationalism and religious conflict most obviously)—for love is generous and fecund; but envy insists on the lovable being that which must be extracted at the expense of the neighbor. Thus, mimetic rivalry is the enemy of God's commandment, and it is the most naturally loveless of acts because it treats everything out of fear, fear of loss and fear of death, which is to say also fear of love and fear of the source of love itself. It is, strictly speaking, the most faithless of conditions.

Loss is the inescapable accomplice of life. That we lose our health, our faculties, our life is the promised end—but the promised end does not end there. For the promise is also held out, that the love we infuse into life will live beyond us, that it will be "as strong as death," as it is said in the *Song of Songs*, and taken up by Franz Rosenzweig in his remarkable work *The Star of Redemption* as the secret of revelation. Such a revelation may or may not be taken in a sense of metaphysical endurance, but its power within life's furtherance is hard to dispute— for the names of the dead are ever a reminder to the future of deeds that are either damnable (deserving of erasure from the future) or veneration, precisely because they have infused the living with something more lovable.

For good and ill, what has shaped the West in turn is no longer confined to the West. I live in Hong Kong and I hear the troubadours as much in the canto pop songs here as in the pop songs in North America or Italy. Likewise, the skyscrapers here are every bit as indebted to the principles of mechanism as the bridges in Europe or Australia. Yet, of course, love is polyphonous and its global shapes endless and far from isomorphic. This book is but a sketch of some of its major spirits which transformed the West. One thing, though, that is worth emphasizing is that while I argued in *Power, Love and Evil* that love is a complex spirit that responds to being summoned and a force which takes hold of people—hence it is frequently divinized (though often that divinization emphasizes different aspects so that, for example, Eros and Aphrodite are not simply equated)—the Jews and the Christians were, at least in terms of the tradition that was to form the West, the first to elevate its importance to the greatest of divine commands.[2] And the West is very much how it is because of that particular command—albeit, the West is also a consequence of the breakage of the command, the countless falls from grace, the flights from God's love, the violation of the divine requirement to love that neighbor, who as Franz Rosenzweig emphasized in his biblical translation, we should love because the neighbor, like us, is like Him, we are all in His image.

Notes

1. The same premise is at work in my *Power, Love and Evil: Contribution to a Philosophy of the Damaged* (Amsterdam and New York: Rodopi, 2008), which can be seen as a companion volume to this work.
2. In China, Mozi (late fifth to early fourth century BCE) taught a doctrine of universal love, but his influence seems to have not been widespread.

Acknowledgments

I wish to thank Lou, Betty, Tony, and Ann Cristaudo, Jennifer Buckley, Lelani B. Paras, Paul Caringella, Michael Morrisey, Robert Hamerton-Kelly, Matt del Nevo, and Heung-wah (Dixon) Wong.

Introduction

Our stories of gods and God and, for the most part, of life are love stories, attempts to make sense of love as the ground and/or end of life. Of course, there have been other grounds and ends, but, in the Western world at least, no attempt to give a meaning to life has been quite as compelling. And now, in a time and place when gods and God seem spent forces, signs that merely deflect back upon the frightened and the superstitious, it is not that we have wanted to part company with love. On the contrary, our atheistic culture was born out of a desire to let love roam free from the encrustations of fear. The mechanistic world may have been a silent one in its origin, but it too was invented/discovered by lovers. The greatest surviving exposition of the atomistic view of nature from the ancients, Lucretius' *The Way Things Are*, is not only a sustained lyric, but it is written under supplication to Venus. That is to say, Lucretius who sees and stands (with Epicurus's original insight) that "Too many times/Religion mothers crime and wickedness," presents his story of nature in the context of an invocation to the goddess of love and a dedication to a man, Memmius.[1] In spite of Lucretius's intention to show us the truth and power of nature, and that nature, in its smallest elements, is the everlasting condition of the real, and not the will of the gods, the truth is disclosed through speech and that speech is undertaken in service to love. The paradox, mentioned in almost every edition of *The Way Things Are*, that a god is invoked at the beginning of the poem which will disclose that the gods themselves are the products of nature, of the atoms, and hence, unlike nature do not hold sway over us, points to the fact that while the ground of our being may be the tiniest particles which make up nature, even the early mechanists felt that our nature longs for love. Love, for Lucretius, while not being the ground of existence is, nevertheless, the end of existence. Lucretius' opening prayer is distinctly in the tradition of Empedocles, the pre-Socratic philosopher who claimed that the cosmos is the product of love and

1

strife. For Empedocles and Lucretius, benign relationships within nature are love relationships, and thus Lucretius prays that the goddess pour herself around Mars, so that he and his fellow Romans may live in peace, that is, in the state of love. In keeping with the sensibility that had become a fairly widespread reaction to the cruel grotesqueness of Roman licentiousness, Lucretius sought to persuade his readers of the dangers of sex. He had preserved the doctrine of the two Aphrodites which Plato had identified in the *Symposium* and Iamblichus had later named the fair and dark eros.

Lucretius is an expression of the depth of the need that places us under love's sign even in the act of the pursuit of knowledge of the nature of things. This is also true of the communication that is communion, of the speech with nature about the nature of nature so that we can foster our nature in as good a way as possible. Within the Roman Empire and its aftermath, faith in a loving God had far wider social appeal than nature's building blocks. Naturalism would have to wait until the power of Christian symbols had fallen into widespread disrepute because they were widely perceived as too often deployed for the masking of sheer power and worldly evil. But as with the example of Lucretius, the return of naturalism quickly found those who made nature compatible with love's reign. The emergence of the libertine as a type in the eighteenth century was as much the obvious manifestation that nature's worshippers would find their way to love as Spinoza's *Ethics* is a love story whose central truth is that:

> The intellectual love of the mind towards God is that very love of God whereby God loves himself, not in so far as he is infinite, but in so far as he can be explained through the essence of the human mind regarded under the form of eternity; in other words, the intellectual love of the mind towards God is part of the infinite love wherewith God loves himself.[2]

What Spinoza conceived as totality is, with some philosophical exceptions, generally fractured into the sovereign subjects which constitute modern men and women. But the cry for love is no less, and remains no less once God has died or the gods have fled. The vital significance of living speech which Spinoza downplays, but which was fundamental to Lucretius's naturalism is revived by Sigmund Freud, who brings mechanism back into the fold of the erotic search that drives it and the human voice that speaks it. Like Spinoza and Epicurus, Freud takes the polarities of meaning as pain and pleasure, the former of which he equates with the thwarting of the libidinal drive which he sees as the essential determination of our nature. Freud's genitally focused narrative was always too one-sided, too indifferent to the different stages and callings of life to contain psychology as such.[3] Not surprisingly, his best students would fall out with him precisely on this issue. However, one may view Freud's account of the oedipal complex or the stages of development and the causes of neurosis; it is noteworthy that he himself thought one of his greatest insights was when he managed to see beyond the pleasure principle and found the struggle between the life drive (eros) and the death drive (the demonic).

While Freud's reduction of the religious stage of humanity to the expression of the superego finds as little sympathy among serious theologians as it does support among atheistic social theorists, there is a moment where one can see that Freud's vision of nature and of the purpose of life and world making here is no different in essence from that of the great religions of love or neo-Platonism. As he writes in *Civilization and its Discontents*, "civilization is a process in service of Eros, whose purpose is to combine single human individuals, and after that families, then races, peoples and nations, into one great unity, the unity of mankind."[4]

Psychoanalysis is intended to be the means for the facilitation of this promise. The "speaking cure" of therapy is meant to enable men and women to overcome the arrestation of their development that is caused by their guilt. However substantial may be one's disagreements with Freud; almost all of Freud's exaggerations and obsessions are the price he paid to redeem the sexual energy from the calumny it endured for so long—that calumny was itself a reaction to its widespread loveless deployment in the service of cruelty and the death instinct (in pre-Christian Rome) by those who enslaved others and used them solely for their own pleasure. After Freud, the West has been able again to talk honestly and openly about the role that sexuality plays in love. The development of twentieth and twenty-first centuries has been one in which Freud's sexually all-pervasive concept of eros has given way to an understanding of childhood and adult development in which love is of central importance. Concomitantly, the role of sexuality can only be rightly gauged if seen in the light of love's power. Such discourses that break down the myths and fears continue in Freud's tracks of demystifying sexuality and creating bonds of understanding between people of different sexual proclivities and variations. At the heart of that understanding is dialogue. In the first instance, the dialogue was, for Freud, that between analyst and analysand. How many need this and how effective it is as a practice is open to arguments based on experience. But what is less contentious is that Freud opened up the community to dialogue about its own desires and practices.

Nevertheless, when sexuality becomes the end of existence, it becomes but one more sad and dangerous myth to replace the modern myth of romantic marriage: for nothing that can be outgrown can be the end; and even sexual longing must give way, or eventually be torn away in life/death. But that loss need not be, and is not, love's loss. The key to the expansion of the human heart, one important to Freud, and taken up by Jacques Lacan, for whom the unconscious is structured like a language, is the opening up of dialogue between all: the articulation of the desires and hungers and mad possessions, the entire gamut of the lack, and the collision between that lack as the Real and what Lacan calls the Symbolic (that concatenation of socially accepted enclaves and practices in which we function). Each is caught up in his or her own drives/desires/fantasies and only through our acknowledging this can we continue in the process of love's union. This is not to deny that there are times when sexual longings/needs look very small indeed besides what the moment calls for. But these needs also have their moments of calling and hence Venus will not endure being banished forever, even when she bears the blame for the world having become so cruel that only the sign of a God-man suffering on a cross can bring it back to its sense of love, or when the world has become so mechanized and abstract that she too dissolves into the material particles of the machine.

Love is a power which dissolves the lover and makes a re-creation of the self possible. The self is constantly remade through its loves. That is why Augustine stressed the importance of what we love. Loving the wrong object, i.e., loving that which will destroy us, does indeed dissolve us equally as much as loving that which will make us more whole or complete, or, in theological terms, more in keeping with the divine in whose image we are made. But such love does little good—it is, as Augustine said, the source of evil.

Mass evil or the great socially violent contagions, which spread mimetically and which require some outlet lest the entire society self-destruct, are all fueled by the wrong loves. The more overtly Christian Girard's thesis became, the more this became evident in his work. Girard is not primarily interested in the who or the what of desire, but in the mimetic rivalry that takes hold irrespective of either who desires or what is desired. And his recognition that the more typical means of locating and sacrificing a victim who would bear all the "sins" of the world doom societies to an eternal return of imitative desire, violence, and sacrifice. The Christian innovation is not in the overturning of mimesis—we are mimetic creatures, and this is evident in the most fundamental modes of social reproduction from parenting to schooling to civil society and to political institutions. Nor does it, as Girard seems to have somewhat belatedly realized, involve eliminating the relationship between love and the sacrificial as such. Rather it is the nature or quality of what we mean by sacrifice and the love that acts as a circuit breaker to the contagion—a willingness to be the sacrifice oneself and not seek someone else to take on the role of the sacrificial victim, while recognizing that the demand to find a sacrifice is alien to God's loving nature—that was the specifically Christian innovation. That innovation is behind the most authentic of Christian types, the real witness, the martyr. This is the most powerful faith in love—one even more powerful than the certainty of resurrection itself—as exemplified in the account of Jesus's own deep sense of forsakenness on the cross. For even crying out in a moment of total forsakenness, of the overwhelming sense of nothing other than death, the love that led to the cross is never renounced. If men are so lacking in love and so lost that they think they need sacrifice, then God Himself must be the sacrifice—that is the great Christian understanding of love. And it arises out of the realization that love stands in the closest relationship to evil. Girard tends to talk of violence rather than evil, though violence is but evil at the moment it is unveiled. Evil is always violation, always on the way to violence, always the attempted extinction of loving life.

If this book provides a chronological account of love in the Western world, this is not meant to suggest that each new understanding of love is superior to what precedes it. The spirits of love I am talking about are "dispatched," discovered, or created as they are needed. They are each responses to a crisis, to a great contagion of catastrophe that forces the heart to be open to another way to love. The Christian (and here again it is deeply indebted and reliant upon Jewish insights) understanding of the Father, the loving God, who as the loving source also posits a loving end of existence, its salvation is, I think, the most profound spirit of all love's spirits. And so important is it that those other innovations and spirits of love have significance and power to the extent that they cooperate with it.

The understanding of love that evolved first with Judaism but was further developed, elaborated upon, and universalized with Christianity is ever in danger of being lost. And it does not seem to me that people who call themselves Christians are either more deserving or even desirous of the kind of love that Christianity has uncovered. It is a serious question whether the majority of Western Christians really understand their faith, or whether under its various signs and symbols they have substituted more idolatrous and "natural" urges and goals—for while Christianity (and Judaism) disclose something true about life and love, it is far from obvious that these truths are natural, whatever that term may mean. What requires cultivation is not "natural" and love—and our understanding of it—most definitely requires cultivation, a clearance of other natural beckonings and possibilities. Western men and women are the most rootless of all creatures. This rootlessness stands in the closest relationship to their freedom. While freedom is along with equality the most important of all modern social values, it is questionable whether most people really flourish with their freedom. By saying that freedom is not an end in itself, I do not want to surreptitiously introduce an argument for rule by a technocratic elite or despot—far from it, that is where we are dangerously heading. But it does need to be emphasized that freedom is the gap between bondages—our participation in life is one in which we are bound to our undertakings. Thus, we may change our undertakings, but that does not mean that what we have undertaken will sever its bonds with us simply because we wish to sever the bond. Were that not the case, criminals would not find their past coming back to haunt them in the form of prosecutions and jail sentences. Our freedom is but a moment within the various bindings and services—our various loves, which are our bonds—which constitute our life. All of this was widely understood within premodern Christian nations.

Those of us who have been born into or dwell into formally Christian nations rarely realized how Christianized we have been. I am not so much interested in whether people reembrace the rituals and symbols of this Christian heritage. But I think it important that they grasp the potency that is part of their own past, especially when like everything belonging to the past that potency is diminished by oblivion. Why I think it important is because it offers something profound for the establishment of human solidarity—and this it seems to me was the great achievement of Christianity—that it insisted that all, even our enemies, are God's children, our neighbors, and our future—the question is whether that future is heavenly or hellish.

Notes

1. Lucretius, *The Way Things Are*, trans. Rolfe Humphries (Bloomington, IN: Indiana University Press, 1969), 22.
2. Benedictus de Spinoza, *The Ethics* in *On the Improvement of the Understanding/The Ethics/Correspondence, The Chief Works of Benedict de Spinoza, Volume 2*, trans. R.H.M. Elwes, (New York: Dover, 1955), prop. XXXVI, pt. V.
3. Even the love between family members (parents for children and vice versa, love between siblings) is "aim-inhibited love." Sigmund Freud, *Civilization and Its Discontents*, trans. Joan Riviere (London: Hogarth, 1973), 39.
4. *Civilization and Its Discontents*, 59.

1

Plato and the First Philosophy of Love

The evolution of the West is, inter alia, a synthesis of three main loves: love of wisdom (philosophy), love of God (the church), and romantic love, which eventually becomes the basis of the modern family and the source of endless "entertainment."

To be sure, love of wisdom has largely dissipated now into science and administration, love of God into the means whereby the neighbor is not treated as an inferior or exploited. Romance has still largely been encapsulated in the marriage partner/life partner, although the large numbers of marriage breakdowns make a reassessment of that myth, and a more open and honest account of the needs and truth behind it, as pressing for us as it was for Flaubert, whose *Madame Bovary* so beautifully shows that romance is one of the last and most durable myths of the modern.

All forms of the expression of love are love's means, not its ends: this is as true of God as it is of philosophy, as it is of the family. Love is violated whenever the form for the activation of love is taken as the source of love itself. Of course, the fundamental idea of designating love as the God, as the one God of love was meant to enable men and women to never lose their way. The name and the simplicity of his command was meant to keep ever alive the value and wonder of serving love. But it is impossible for us not to lose our way. And the name that activates so much glory, by that very fact inevitably finds itself covered in deeds of shame by those who fail to live up to love's requirements, either through the rigidity and dogmatism and shortsightedness of their own understanding or else through their preference for more immediate ends, which have to do with loves that no longer care for the neighbor and the kingdom to come. The heart is what we take to heaven, and the futurity of heaven—the endless deferral unto death—makes it easy for the heart to follow a more immediate goal.

9

The moment human beings developed a method for their love of wisdom, philosophy was born. From philosophy the techniques for a systematic ordering of our understanding of the soul, the polity, nature, and the cosmos were first set out. The Western modalities of the organization of knowledge (which itself leads to an expansion of some types of knowledge) are fundamentally philosophical. Our technological and administrative and legal systems owe their potency to the systemic capacity that is philosophy's greatest achievement—an achievement which is very general, and yet far greater than any single philosophical solution to any philosophical question. It was philosophy that created the university, philosophy that created theology, philosophy that enabled the systemization of legal codes (hence the enormous significance of the application of Aristotelian reasoning to the rediscovered Justinian law Code),[1] philosophy that created the entire re-view of the structure of nature. In his *Logic*, Hegel had noted that the extent of the gamut of philosophy can be gauged not only from the fact that Newton was considered to be a great philosopher, but that the name of philosopher went down "as far as the price list of instrument makers." "All instruments, such as the thermometer and barometer," he continued, "are styled philosophical instruments."[2]

Just as the breakthrough in modern science was seen as a philosophical breakthrough, so were the breakthroughs in modern systems of government—breakthroughs to be sure which built upon historical contingencies, but which, nevertheless, received important refinements by Locke, Montesquieu, and Rousseau that came to be inserted in the constitutions of the United States and France. Even Adam Smith's case for economic efficiency being grounded in the free market was a philosophical argument which he developed while being employed as a professor of moral philosophy. But love is far older than philosophy, and philosophy is but one of its branches. Though love's shards are everywhere, the love that finds its way into philosophy is a Greek love.

Even before the Greeks had written records of the gods' presence, they had stone figures of worship. We might say that the capacity to range between earth's stone and the gods' who dwell in heaven points to the infinite power of the human imagination. Poetry had, however, been called to follow the song that moved through everything, including stones. Thus, in his *The Goddess of Love: The Birth, Triumph, Death and Return of Aphrodite*, Geoffrey Grigson speaks of the origin of the goddess of love, Aphrodite, long before she appears as an epic character: "She began as a conical stone, as if the symbol and the weight of a blind urge."[3]

Aphrodite begins as a blind urge. But all the Greek gods display what Bernard Knox has called their "furious self-absorption." "Each one," he continues:

> is a separate force which, never questioning or examining the nature of its own existence, moves blindly, ferociously, to the affirmation of its will in action…. To be a god is to be totally absorbed in the exercise of one's own power, the fulfill-ment of one's own nature, unchecked by any thought of others except as obstacles to be overcome; it is to be incapable of self-questioning or self-criticism.[4]

If Aphrodite does first appear as stone, it is suggestive of her relativity in the scheme of things, as is the fact that in Hesiod her birth is the result of Cronos having castrated his father, Ouranos, and throwing his testicles into the sea. She is born out of the foam that gathers around them in the sea. In other words, love is originally for the Greeks, a power born of other forces, not the source of creation.

The earliest fully developed philosophical expositions on love that we have are, of course, from Plato. In the *Symposium*, he indicates just how important he considers love to be, first by having Socrates say that "love is the one thing in the world I understand" (*Symposium* 177d) and second, by having the character, Eryximachus, complain that "not one single poet has ever sung a song in praise of so ancient and so powerful a god as love."[5] That is a very strong claim, and while it is open to dispute (Sappho, for example) it does alert us to the fact that Plato does think that he is dealing with a neglected force. Certainly the epic and, what we have of the tragic and comic traditions are far from offering paeans to love. For example, much of the *Iliad* deals with the power of love in one shape or other. But love is far from represented as a great good, and whereas the *Symposium* celebrates eros, in Homer it is love under the auspices of Aphrodite which occupies most of his attention. Moreover, through Homer we see what significance can be drawn from Aphrodite's relationship to war. The evil of the Trojan War is born out of love, of the erotic love between Helen and Paris. It is the impropriety of love which tears apart kingdoms and households. Paris "offended Athena and Hera—both goddesses./ When they came to his shepherd's fold he favored Love/ who dangled before his eyes the lust that loosed disaster" (*Iliad* 24:31–36). Aphrodite is an affront because she is a transgressive goddess. Athena, the protectress of cities and the bearer of urban manners, was offended because Paris had succumbed to a power that threatened to tear apart civility. Hera, the jealous wife of Zeus, was angry because Aphrodite tears husbands from their duty, thus leaving a wife vulnerable to warriors seeking booty. Hera's and Athena's hatred of the Trojans is a hatred of the energy (of Aphrodite) that leads men to violate the most fundamental law of civility toward strangers in peacetime. The destruction of Troy stems from Paris's enchantment that led to the violation of that code of civility. Yet the power of this love and the potency of the beauty which causes it is so intoxicating that the old chiefs of Troy, when they get a glimpse of Helen "moving along the ramparts/...murmured to one another, gentle, winged words: Who on earth could blame them? Ah no wonder the men of Troy and Argives under arms have suffered years of agony all for her, for such a woman. Beauty, terrible beauty!" (*Iliad* 3:185–90). And Hera herself so single-minded in her animosity to the Trojans knows that the powers of Aphrodite can conquer even the will of the strongest of the gods. In her desire to manipulate Zeus, Hera asks for extra powers from Aphrodite. "Give me love," she says, "give me Longing now, the powers/ you use to overwhelm all gods and mortal men!" (*Iliad* 14:421–22). And Aphrodite "loosed from her breasts the breastband,/ pierced and alluring, with every kind of enchantment/ woven through it. There is the heat of Love,/ the pulsing rush of Longing. The love's whisper/ irresistible—magic to make the sanest man go mad" (*Iliad* 14:257–61).

But there are many layers of love in the *Iliad* besides the sheer power of sensuous beauty cast by Aphrodite: the *Iliad* demonstrates the love between husband and wife (nothing in the *Iliad* is more touching than the great scene on the ramparts between Andromache and Hector), just as it demonstrates love of fathers for their children, of comrades in arms, of love for the fatherland. And even though Briseis is but Achilles's slave, Achilles can say: "Are they the only men alive who love their wives,/ those sons of Atreus? Never! Any decent man,/ a man with a sense, loves his own, cares for his own as deeply as I, I loved that woman with all my heart,/ though I won her as a trophy with my spear..." (*Iliad* 9:413–17). Indeed, it is no exaggeration to say that the *Iliad* is finally a tale not only of the danger and victory of Achilles's rage but of love which lifts men above.

Achilles's refusal to fight is overcome by his love of Patroclus and the further rage that he incurs with Patroclus's death; Priam's love for his son elevates his courage so that he will sneak into the Achaeans camp and implore Achilles to bury his son. Achilles, who says when Hector asks to swear a pact before the gods with him, that the victor will guarantee burial rites to the defeated, "don't talk to me of pacts./ There are no binding oaths between men and lions/ wolves and lambs can enjoy no meeting of the minds/ they are all bent on hating each other to the death./ So with you and me. No love between us. No truce" (*Iliad* 22:309–13) changes his mind when he sees Priam face to face. The love which has raised Priam touches Achilles. Pity can only be expressed once the two have a common bond. Their mutual agony caused by their loss of their loved one is the link between these two men. That shared agony creates the space in the heart that rage only fills insufficiently. The animal in man bows before the love in man and the sign of this love is the concession of the burial rite. Death, as painful as it is, is far less painful than the knowledge that a loved one is left to nature's elements and predators to be just a carcass like some animal.

Homeric love is always implicated in violence. And this is equally as evident in the *Odyssey* as the *Iliad*. The slaughter of the suitors at the end of the *Odyssey* is the slaughter of a loving husband protecting his property and avenging the humiliation of his wife, his son, and family name. If Odysseus's name was ever associated with ending the Trojan War through the ingenious act of duplicity behind the creation of the Trojan horse, it was equally associated with the tenacity of his love which enabled him to avoid the entrapments which would leave Penelope and Telemachus the victims of the desires of strangers. It is only by combining his heroism and nimble wits (the man of nimble wits is his Homeric epithet) with his role as avenger that he is the complete man—unlike Achilles, Odysseus is not just a man of the past, not just someone who exists for war, but also for peace. But Odysseus is no more able to end violence than Achilles; not only that but through their loves both invariably fuel violence.

It is no exaggeration to say that the single-most overwhelming problem that confronts Plato and Socrates is the seemingly ceaseless violence of the world they inherited. The immediate backdrop to Plato is Socrates's execution, but the larger backdrop to both men is the Peloponnesian war and the violence between the Athenian dictatorship and the democracy. All of Plato's incursions into politics are an attempt to find the harmony that Athens has lacked under dictatorship and democracy. And while a number of twentieth-century critics such as Popper and I. F. Stone highlighted how antidemocratic Plato was, the fact is that from his perspective the difference between the dictatorship and democracy was not so clear cut—the dictatorship threatened to kill Socrates, the democracy did so. Thus, did he seek to find a basis for politics which could avoid the pathologies of tyranny and democracy.

Along Girardian lines, one might add that Plato fathomed that the violence endemic to tyranny and democracy was due to their mimetic madness. The mimetic link between tyranny and democracy is most clearly brought out by Plato in the *Gorgias* where he argues that the most important capacity (he refuses to honor this "occupation of a shrewd and enterprising spirit" with the word art [*Gorgias* 463]) for winning power in the democracy, rhetoric, is the means by which the soul gradually deteriorates as it imitates the imitator who has already lost any proper sense of truth.[6] Thus, he has the urbane teacher of oratory, Gorgias, who seems to be completely oblivious to the psychic poison he is spreading, be followed in ascending order of degeneracy and shamelessness by Polus and Callicles. After having demonstrated that Gorgias himself wants to teach what is right and just, but is unable to do so because he only knows how to teach the "routines" of rhetoric, he enters into discussion with Polus who is learning from Gorgias how to command a crowd. The issue, for Socrates, is what he will sway them for. For Polus, it is self-evident that orators are "the most powerful in their cities" (*Gorgias* 466b), and that means, "like tyrants, [being able] to put to death any man they will, and deprive of their fortunes and banish whoever it seems best" (*Gorgias* 466b–c). Further, Polus is puzzled that Socrates would not want to become a tyrant, for being a tyrant he could do whatever he wills, mainly to do what one pleases, which means "to kill, to exile and to follow my own pleasure in every act" (*Gorgias* 469c). In the course of defending oratory, Polus has found himself defending the life of tyranny, and to prove his point that the tyrant is happy he takes the case of Archelaus, the son of a slave woman. Had he acted justly, Polus points out, he would still be a slave, but he sent for his master and uncle,

> ostensibly to restore to him the power of which Perdiceas [his father and the brother of Alcetas] had deprived him, and then entertained the man and his son. Alexander, who was his own cousin and about his own age, and after making them drunk he flung them into a wagon, took them away by night, and made away with them by murder...a little later, so far from wishing to become happy by justly bringing up the rightful heir to the throne, his own brother,

the legitimate son of Perdiceas, a child of about seven years, and restoring the throne to him, he threw him into a well and drowned him, and then told the child's mother, Cleopatra, that the boy had fallen in and killed himself while chasing a goose. ...and I suppose there are other Athenians besides yourself who would prefer to be any Macedonian rather than Archelaus. (*Gorgias* 471)

For Polus, then, it is self-evident that this kind of behavior far from being something that the Athenians would find repellant is a source of envy. What Polus reveals as the real objective of oratory—to assist one in being able to become a tyrant—is also held to be the case of that kindred pseudoart or "knack," sophistry, in the *Theages*, a dialogue which may not have been written by Plato but whose sensibility is thoroughly Platonic. In that dialogue Theages is led by Socrates to concede in passing that he might pray to become a tyrant "as I think you and everyone else would."[7] Mark Joyal in his commentary and critical edition of the *Theages* states that the idea that happiness is personified in the tyrant was a belief that Greeks probably shared, and in the popular imagination tyrants stood only one step below the gods.[8]

Unlike Callicles, whom Ancient rumor had it may have been Plato's depiction of his future self had he not met Socrates, both Theages and Polus are prone to the great social mechanism of shame. And thus, while if circumstances perhaps enabled them to be tyrants, they would indeed have become the murderers and pillagers they admire, deprived of opportunity, they go along with the demos' (or the weak if we follow Callicles) more conventional moral evaluations. In the case of Polus, Socrates is able to get him to agree to the argument that it is better to be wronged than do wrong—an argument completely at odds with his earlier position. This only serves to show how desire is mimetic and how a man like Polus could just as easily end up a just man as a tyrant—everything depends upon who he imitates. Indeed, this is the whole point of philosophy for Plato, that it is the one practice which imitates what is most valuable and good—the good itself. The philosopher pursues the eternal forms because they, unlike the confused opinions of the mob, and the confused representations of people who have imitated confused imitators (the orators, sophists, and poets) who deal in shadow realities, provide what is genuinely worthy of imitation. And this is also why in the *Republic*, Plato presents the dramatic imitation of Socrates in the person of Glaucon, who is the one discussant who can follow him all the way into an understanding not only of the good city, and the good life, but who understands how important it is to see that the cosmic order is also just. If one does not bother imitating the best, one might very well be imitating the worst. Though Plato goes even further—the real alternative is between the life of a philosopher or a tyrant. For it is those poles that provide the starkest models to be imitated. The average man who is caught in-between reason and passion, who now and then has true opinions only to lose them to a more cloudy and dangerous view of life, has no real control over his life. The tyrant has the least control but at least he gets what he wants—the absolute appearance of the good, the phantasmic which will ultimately devour him. The tyrant is a tyrant by virtue of being ready to do anything to achieve his desire, but he seals his doom for Plato because he shows another how to be a tyrant. If a tyrant could completely love and pleasure himself, he might be able to escape the ever possible end that awaits him—being murdered by whom he desires. Either, the tyrant will be overthrown by someone just like him, or, what is not much better, live pent up, needing to observe every plot and conspiracy, never knowing who to trust, in perpetual fear of that very occurrence (cf. *Gorgias* 510–11; *Republic* 511ff.).

It has often been argued that the *Republic* is an anti-utopian work, particularly (though not only) by Leo Strauss and those of his school, and that the political ideas of the *Republic* that deal with political and social organization and control are being held up to ridicule by their inventor. The fact that Plato suggests the city be handed over to ten-year olds strongly suggests that the philosophically ruled city will be impossible to realize. Yet, I think that to concede the ideal city is impossible to actualize is a very different issue from the idea that he does not really believe in the *value* of the political ideas expressed therein. What I think interpreters like Leo Strauss and his student Allan Bloom who run this argument neglect is the dire nature of the social and political realities confronted by Plato. The very fact that he would return to the problem of founding a city and providing a constitution in such elaborate detail as he does in *The Laws* is indicative, I think, of the urgency behind Plato's political writings. Plato's own writings on politics from the argument that philosophers should be kings to his philosophically detailed outlined constitution (which would be a mixed constitution) are all motivated by the terrifying brutality and overwhelming failure of the Greek city states. Plato's unusual fusion of conservative and radical political instincts all stem from this crisis. And indeed his preference for Sparta over Athens comes from the fact that the Spartans have a degree of constraint and control lacking in the more pleasure-seeking democratic Athenians. In general, though, he sees that whatever constitutional type holds sway it is doomed eventually to gravitate to tyranny. That bleakness of the inherent degeneracy of the city state closely reflects his deep despair at the pandemonium, evident in its external and internal violence, of the Athenian demos. Ultimately the tendency to tyranny, for Plato, springs from the sacrifice of reason to desire and desire to pleasure. As he depicts it, the center of Athenian political life, the assembly, is little more that a crowd ever bordering on frenzy who are mimetically swayed by the orators and students of sophistry. They will, as he points out in the *Gorgias*, turn as swiftly on their greatest statesmen such as Pericles as they will applaud them when they are sufficiently pandered to (*Gorgias* 515ff). Further, as we have suggested, the problem of mimetic violence is compounded for Plato by what in the ancient world was the peculiar social role of what Plato designated as the mimetic "arts" which feed the frenzied desires of the mob, viz. rhetoric, sophistry, and poetry. Plato devoted a number of dialogues (especially the *Protagoras, Sophist, Cratylus, Ion, Euthydemus*, and *Republic*) as well as the *Gorgias* to showing his readers their nature and dangers, while pointing out why philosophy must not be confused with them.

In the *Republic*, Plato dwells upon the relationship between violence and poetry and it would be no exaggeration to say that just as the *Republic* offers the ultimate choice between the lives of the philosopher and the tyrant, it also offers the choice between a way that leads to harmony and one that enflames the emotions, but which Plato thinks, drags one into tyranny, viz. poetry. Thus, does Plato tear into Homer and Hesiod and the dramatic poets. The entire critique of the poets is based around the fact that they are enmeshed in imitation, and it stretches from their depiction of gods and heroes. Specifically, the poets represent gods and heroes who are the real imitators of human beings who have no control over their passions and feelings, and then they present gods and heroes as the highest models worthy of imitation. For Plato, only philosophy has the method to present the right model to take Athens out of the hell it has made of itself.

In sum, then, the major motivation behind Plato can be depicted in terms of imitation—imitation of what is bad by people (poets, etc.) who do not know what the good is—and violence, the never ending explosions of violence that come from each blindly seeking appetitive satisfaction, at least when they have the opportunity to do so, when the thin veneer of social shame is rent apart. The solution is wisdom, and not just any wisdom, wisdom that comes from following the path of reason itself. Reason is part of the soul and orders the cosmos, but it is also beyond the everyday world of flux and appearances. And the depth of belief in the solution is a symptom of the novelty of the solution—it had not been tried. Philosophy, threatened by poets, who did not want their role as the privileged educators of Greece, and by statesmen (another shady lot for Plato), who did not want their role as guiding the more immediate matters of political life, was new. And it was a convenient scapegoat for the problems of Greece. Socrates was the scandal of the Greeks, the scandal who did not believe in the gods, yet believes in strange new gods (a contradiction not seeming to worry his accusers, as Socrates himself points out), the scandal who corrupted the youth. And most scandalous of all, he refused to accept his role as the *skandalon*—had he done so he could have lived. It was precisely this refusal that transformed a small majority of those who found him guilty into an overwhelming majority of those who insisted on the death penalty.

This is the background against which Plato discusses love. And as I will suggest from the outset, his discussion of love is inseparable from the privileged role that he gives to knowledge, a role that stems from his belief that the imitators do not know what it is they are imitating, who simply lack the knowledge to imitate the good, and thus to use another formulation of Plato's, are evil because they are ignorant.

In the *Symposium* and the *Phaedrus*, Plato undertakes a great philosophical analysis of and paean to love, the like of which had never been undertaken before. One philosopher, Empedocles, had made love, along with strife, a fundamental polar force of the cosmos, but Plato does not mention this in the *Symposium*, although one can discern resemblances between Empedocles's naturalistic insights into love and the position that Plato ascribes to Eryximachus who sees love as the harmonizing force in nature. The harmony which nature is able to achieve, it achieves because love brings the natural parts together. For Eryximachus, medicine is the science of what the body loves and medicine is under the sole direction of the god of love. Nature is in search of harmony, and love is the force that brings the disunion into union. Sickness, like evil, is the deviation from harmony. The body is a system in which the parts are drawn to each other, and the healthy body is drawn to what is good for it. It is the doctor's task to know the good for the body and to grasp what really nourishes, what really sustains and produces harmony. The doctor "is to reconcile the jarring elements

of the body and force them, as it were, to fall in love with each other."
(*Symposium* 186d). In this way the science of medicine is likened to
that of music (gymnastics and agronomy are also said to be under the
direction of love). But given the subordination that nature has under
the sway of the idea, for Plato, Eryximachus's thoughts on love are
not developed in the serious manner that those of Socrates are in the
two dialogues, the *Phaedrus* and the *Symposium*. And as in so many
things, although Plato's analysis on the surface reaches conclusions
which seem to belong strictly to him, yet at another level he reaches
the inevitable conclusions of any genuine philosophical investigation
on the topic. In both dialogues the culmination of the discussion of
love is the comprehension or intellectual vision of the idea. The lover
of wisdom for Plato is the lover of the ideas, and although Plato's on-
tology has found few supporters among the great philosophers of the
West, yet he does express something fundamentally true of philosophy:
philosophers are indeed in love with ideas, ideas (how and wherever
we may wish to locate their origins) are what draw one to philosophy,
are what philosophers engage with, are what philosophers teach to
students and debate with each other, and are what philosophers allow themselves to be consumed by. Wisdom is only comprehensible
throughout the entire philosophical tradition via the ideas which our
reason can grasp. Philosophers, we may say, love reasoning, even if,
as Schelling, Nietzsche, Heidegger and their epigoni have done and
do; they are reasoning about the limits of reason and the primacy of
something/mystery/power/Being that is unreasonable. Plato had argued in the *Sophist* that identity and difference pertain to every idea.
And even when a philosopher like Martin Heidegger who insists he
is overcoming Platonism deploys a term such as Being which is supposed to escape being a mere idea, the Platonic henchmen of identity
and difference force the term to take its place in the realm of ideas as
soon as it is discussed. Anything we discuss which can be conceptually
demarcated as being different from something else (even if we insist
it is no thing), and anything whose features can be seen as pertaining
to, and identical with something (even if metaphorically or merely
analogically) are inevitably absorbed into (the Platonic mould)of an
idea. Philosophers may not like conceding this to Plato, but this is
the price they pay for not being content to be poets, and for having
entered a certain plane of observation and level of conceptual gener-
ality. Even to admire poets and to point philosophy in the direction
of poetry, as Martin Heidegger or Friedrich Nietzsche did, is still not

to be a poet. This is the great power of philosophy generally and the tyranny of Plato who is the philosopher to first write of what is really happening when one thinks rigorously in terms of genus and species and complies with the law of noncontradiction. Thus, almost from its inception, philosophy moves its practitioners away from the tactility of love to the communion of minds, to an immersion in the ideas that may dazzle lovers of wisdom.

It is the nature of love that the lover is immersed in the beloved, and the great danger is that love itself may vanish in the act of immersion. For when one loves the other, the love is always the middle term, but invariably the beloved is seen as the source of love itself. Thus, love is constantly lost/betrayed/and slips away. In the history of philosophy this is no less the case. The wisdom that is the beloved of philosophy all too often takes over so that the very act of love, which is behind the pursuit of wisdom, vanishes. In the history of philosophy, wisdom tends to swallow up or drive out love (periodically having to reassert itself). Thus, for example, wisdom is a classical virtue—in Plato and Aristotle—(the other virtues being justice, courage, and temperance, and sometimes piety), but love is not. And in Plato, wisdom definitely trumps love, but not without Plato having identified some beautiful characteristics of love, which largely follows from his belief that love is the pursuit of the beautiful. For Plato, the beautiful body of the beloved that the body of the lover wants to touch, to participate in, is a reflection of what the soul is truly striving for. Beauty reminds the soul of true being, which the soul has previously encountered (*Phaedrus* 249–51). Eros is the force that drives us toward what we love. We think we love the beloved, but what is really happening is that we are opening ourselves up to qualities latent within us, and as we do this we project what is moving our own soul (and the soul is defined in this dialogue as the source and first principle of motion for all other things that are moved [245–46]). In a passage of striking beauty and enduring power, Socrates elaborates on the point that every lover sees in the beloved an image of the god who rules:

> And so each selects a fair one for his love after his disposition, and even as if the beloved himself were a god he fashions for himself as it were an image, and adorns it to be the object of his veneration and worship.

> Thus the followers of Zeus seek a beloved who is Zeus-like in soul; wherefore they look for one who is by nature disposed to the love of wisdom and the leading of men, and when they have found him and

come to love him they do all in their power to foster that disposition. And if they had not aforetime trodden this path, they now set out upon it, learning the way from any source that may offer or finding it for themselves, and as they follow up the trace within themselves of the nature of their own god their task is made easier, inasmuch as they are constrained to fix their gaze upon him, and reaching out after him in memory they are possessed by him, and from this they take their ways and manners of life, in so far as a man can partake of a god. But all this, mark you, they attribute to the beloved, and the draughts which they draw from Zeus they pour out, like bacchants, into the soul of the beloved, thus creating in him the closest possible likeness to the god they worship.

Those who were in the train of Hera look for a royal nature, and when they have found him they do unto him all things in like fashion. And so it is with the followers of Apollo and each other god. Every lover is fain that his beloved should be of a nature like to his own god, and when he has won him, he leads him on to walk in the ways of their god, and after his likeness, patterning himself thereupon and giving counsel and discipline to the boy. There is no jealousy nor petty spitefulness in his dealings, but his every act is aimed at bringing the beloved to be every whit like unto himself and unto the god of their worship. (*Phaedrus* 252–53)

Rosenstock-Huessy, who is generally a severe critic of Plato, once made the point in one of his undergraduate lectures that it was Mrs. Lincoln who facilitated Abraham becoming the president of the United States because through her love he was able to see a vision of himself which no mirror from himself would have yielded.[9] She saw who he could be because she saw his possibilities and her love activated the possibilities in him. All of us contain powers which are dormant until another living soul can awaken them, just as Mrs. Lincoln transformed a man into a great statesman. The point is the same one that Plato is making. We are each governed by some power and we may not always see it with clarity, but love is that power which pulls our minds and souls to what Christians term a calling, what Plato here calls the god we worship, and what a more secular age calls our own possibilities. We have different natures hence we are drawn to worship different gods. The lover wants to wake up the beloved because the lover wants to worship the god whose image is at work through the beloved. Each is really engaged in fashioning the self in the shape of what it is that one worships. We become what we worship and each soul is, for Plato, on a journey of self-knowledge. That journey, for Plato, is not just restricted to this life time. In a number of dialogues, Plato indicates that he believes that we are immortal souls who occupy a body—the Pythagoreans spoke of the body as being a prison of the soul, and Plato follows them here. The best life is one in which one prepares for death, and philosophy itself is said to be a life in which one practices death. Our human existence, for Plato, is frequently considered within a metaphysical framework where the soul is separate from the body and where it can survive the body and even enter into another body after death and take on another life. The process is a process of purification and it requires that we have knowledge of the highest good, the good itself. The beauty that we see in the beloved is not an end, but the beginning of the process of purification and transfiguration or sublimation of the erotic forces which drive us at first toward the bodily and then toward the divine. Whatever we do, for Plato, we do because we think it is good, and it is the good that all living things are seeking. Plato does not equate God and the good, as Plotinus will later do, rather, Plato has his creator god, the demiurge of the *Timaeus*, himself look to the good. For Plato, there is nothing higher than the good, and it is higher than both beauty and truth: we love them because they are good. We love someone because we think they are good or it is good that we love them; we desire beauty because we think it good; we seek for truth because we believe that truth is good, etc. Love, though, says Plato, clouds our reason, it is madness that is heaven sent (*Phaedrus* 244). And yet it too is the power that can activate us to strive for the good. Yet again, the nature of the force is that it is both bodily and spiritually activating. And in one of his most famous metaphors Plato speaks of the soul as a chariot being driven by two steeds, one white, pure, and spiritually directed, the other carnal, a black bucking horse which would drag the soul into a morass of despair and unfulfillment. The fleetingness of temporal things, the inevitability of the withering of the flesh, the disintegration of appearances, the instability of earthly life, and the passions which come upon us, all for Plato indicate the falsity of making the carnal the end product of love.

Typically, though, Plato looks for love as a source of moral guidance. And in the *Symposium*, the first speaker on love, Phaedrus (drawing on the poetic authority of Hesiod and Acusilaus, and the philosophical authority of Parmenides) claims that (a) love is the oldest of gods and the first worshipped and (b) love makes the lover too ashamed to act in an unworthy manner in front of the beloved. Love, he continues, drives men and women to sacrificial heights. Phaedrus's speech is the one of the very few places where Plato recognizes and acknowledges the truth that would become the centerpiece of Christianity, the sacrificial nature of love.[10] The army of lovers that Phaedrus conjures up—the idea being that each will want to shine in the eyes of his beloved, and each will willingly lay down his life in conflict—"nothing but love will make a man offer his life for another's—and not only man but woman"—this army of lovers is, to put it mildly, a long way from the army of Christian martyrs whose spilled blood served as the consecrated site where churches were first built. But Plato has grasped that love drives people to surrender and that part of love's power is built upon this paradox: that what most fills people with the desire to live also drives them to be willing to surrender their very lives. That Plato does not do more with the idea of sacrifice is, I think, indicative of a fundamental limitation within the Platonic vision, a limitation which is visible in the contrast between philosophical martyrdom and Christian martyrdom. Yet it is also the case that sacrifice is, in spite of the infrequency of Plato's reference to and interpretation of sacrifice, at the very heart of Plato's philosophy. As the *Apology* makes it clear, Socrates's martyrdom is the great event which will alter forever the significance of philosophy. The condemned Socrates issues the warning to his judges and jurors, the Athenian demos: they have guaranteed his future influence and his death will advance the cause of philosophy way beyond what may have happened had he been let alone to continue his gad-flyish behaviors. One of the central realizations of any act of martyrdom is that the power to bring about change may be enhanced through the right death. And this realization is integral not only to Socrates's death but to the act of discipleship exhibited by Plato, who as a witness to this act undertook to save Socrates for future generations by capturing his character in writing. Yet the sacrificial act which gives philosophy a potency it probably would not have had without it remains limited. There is simply no philosophical point in continued repetition of the sacrifice, something that Aristotle realized when he fled the wrath of the Athenians, and decided to spare it the ignominy of murdering another philosopher. The significance of Socratic martyrdom is primarily symbolic, and once the symbol has been established to reproduce the act, as it is reproduced in a sacrament, it has no purpose. While we may stretch things for literary or stylistic purposes and speak of the "rituals" of philosophy, rituals are not what philosophers do or require. Procedures yes, but not rituals. Indeed, Kant's *Religion with the Limits of Reason Alone*, which is pretty typical of the Enlightenment attitude to religion as a vehicle for moral instruction, illustrates where the philosophical approach to ritual must lead: it looks for the truths, which can be better reached through arguments that are congealed in the ritual. Hegel, far more sympathetic than Kant to ritual, does a similar thing (though he expands the content beyond moral instruction) by making ritual equivalent to picture thinking and a step on the way to the conceptual realizations that philosophy may attain.

The act of self-sacrifice, then, is at the very heart of the power of Socratic philosophy, and Plato shows this by making Socrates a willing sacrifice. Further, as the *Gorgias* makes amply clear, Plato rejects any idea of enforcing someone else to be the sacrifice, insisting that it is better to be wronged than to do wrong (*Gorgias* 473–75). Socrates is the sacrifice for the mimetic contagion, and he is so willingly, but not because he believes in the legitimacy of the mimetic outbreak which finds its outlet in the blaming of philosophy, in general, and Socrates, in particular, for Athens's chaos. He will die so that philosophy will have a future, and eventually he hopes that philosophy will be able to stop the process. But he must first be prepared to show the demos that their choice of the sacrificial victim will not end the violence that envelops them. The Christian virtues of faith, hope, and love are the three great invisible powers that make a future possible, and Plato is no less dependent upon them than the Christians were. This is evident as soon as we think of the importance of Plato's faith in Socrates and his philosophy, his love of Socrates and philosophy, and his hope that the pathway blazed by Socrates would be followed in the future. Socrates is the new model of imitation, the new Achilles as is stipulated in the *Apology*. Yet while the majority of Platonic dialogues offer a character to be imitated, Plato is seduced by the promise of the argument leading where it may and thus he emphasizes the importance of the truth of Socrates's argument, as if the man is the totality of his arguments, the logos forming flesh. But if the logos form flesh, philosophy is only one instance of logos, which is why, in spite of all Plato's arguments against poetry and rhetoric, Aristotle cannot follow his master, but must rehabilitate them and show we can learn from them.

The recognition of where self-sacrifice fits into life is one of the most primordial of all recognitions, which is certainly not peculiarly Platonic nor Christian. It is a cross-cultural realization that manifests itself in the commonality of vegetable, animal, and even human sacrifice. But what strikes us is how little reflection Plato makes upon this act. It is there, just as is the recognition by Phaedrus that love drives people to self-sacrifice. I have even suggested that with Socrates's death the sacrifice is central to the power that philosophy is able to draw to itself. Yet, unlike in Christianity where the reenactment of the act of the divine self-sacrifice becomes the central symbol of its rituals and is fundamental to the expansion of its message and the absorption and spread of its power, Plato wants to pass swiftly over the earth and draw us toward the beauty and symmetry of the mind, and in particular the ideas of beauty and the good. Plato is too cultivated to dwell on such things (see below my discussion of Rosenstock-Huessy and Matthew's bad taste); conversely he passes too swiftly over the viscera which is closer to the source of love and the need for human association.

In the *Symposium*, after Phaedrus's speech, sacrifice is left behind as each speaker proceeds to identify and praise love. The speaker who follows Phaedrus, Pausanius, seems to be a well-meaning old pedophile who detests those who merely use younger boys for their pleasure and neglect the duties that are at the heart of the moral code of Greek boy love. His speech provides a valuable insight into the mores and laws that existed in Greece and the Orient in Plato's days. Some states such as Elis and Boetia simply permit boy love, others prohibit it—those that do are said by Pausanius to be despotisms which are equally condemnatory of philosophy and sport as of boy love. "For I suppose," he says, "it does not suit the rulers for their subjects to indulge in high thinking, or in staunch friendship and fellowship, which Love more than anything is likely to beget" (182C). For Pausanius, love is a step in a boy's moral education, and where it does not continue from bodily gratification to intellectual development, it is reprehensible. For Pausanius, there are two kinds of love and two Aphrodites—the elder, sprung from no mother's womb but from the heavens themselves, the Uranian Aphrodite or heavenly Aphrodite, while the other the younger daughter of Zeus, is the earthly Aphrodite. According to Pausanius, no action is bad in itself, it depends on how it is performed, and that is the same with love, one is bad and one good. That which is ruled by the earthly Aphrodite is so indiscriminate, he recounts with horror that it will seek out women as well as boys.

The heavenly love, on the other hand is directed toward intelligence rather than the body, and its discrimination requires that it have "nothing of the female" (181c). It is not that Pausanius is opposed to bodily love or preaching celibacy, but he believes in stability and durability and purity of motive. The lover who will ditch the youth as soon as his youthfulness wanes is reprehended, and Pausanius praises the Athenian law code for prescribing some behaviors such as stipulating a time limit of solicitation, while proscribing others such as acting out of ulterior motives, e.g., financial or political gain, or fear of ill treatment. The practice is part of a moral education, a means of access to the kind of activity of which the *Symposium* itself is an example. It is, according to Pausanius, a long-term commitment in which a pleasure which commences with desire flowers into facilitating a richer development of the soul.

While with Phaedrus we have a speech which suggests what the erotic brings out between equals, with Pausanius we are witnessing a speech which is conscious of the bonds and obligations that are required between unequals. In their own way, each is wanting to draw out what is ethical in the erotic, and each is pointing to what the erotic is capable of drawing out of people, its power to push transcendences, the transcendence of moving beyond what it is that is pushing, the pushing that wants bodily satisfaction yet will institutionally confine it as the lover discovers something more beautiful, more worthy or ennobling—the comrade who wants to radiate before his lover and would find fulfillment in a radiance that required death, and the older man who, in spite of his hunger to embrace the youthful beauty, delights in the more enduring beauty of the achievements of intelligence.

But as elevated as Pausanius's speech seems to be, he is really describing and defending a trading system, the trading of wisdom for sexual gratification, a trade that he expresses thus:

> We must therefore combine these two laws - the one that deals with the love of boys and the one that deals with the pursuit of wisdom and the other virtues - before we can agree with that the youth is justified in yielding to his lover. For it is only when lover and beloved come together each by his own especial law - the former lawfully enslaving himself to the youth he loves, in return for his compliance, the latter lawfully devoting his services to the friend who is helping him to become wise and good - the one sharing his wealth of wisdom and virtue, and the other drawing in his poverty upon his friend for a liberal education - it is then, I say, and only then, when the observance of the two laws coincides, that is it right for the lover to have his way. (*Symposium* 184d)

The trade-off of education for sexual favors seems as natural and healthy to Pausanius as it seems unnatural within Christendom, and as politically incorrect (even allowing for the academic respectability and institutional refuge of transgressive sexuality studies) as it does today. Generally the knowledge–sex/eros trading system of Pausanius is one which Plato had seemed to accept for most of his life before attacking it in *The Laws* where he bans homosexuality completely. Later in the *Symposium*, when the drunken Alcibiades breaks in on the party and sings his love of Socrates, Socrates can be contrasted with Pausanius's ideal lover. And the marked contrast is that unlike Pausanius, for Socrates the communion with the soul is its own trade-off; there need not be any spilling of his seed for a fruitful union, as is evident from the tale told by the very desirable Alcibiades, who relates the story of how, wanting to be taken by Socrates, he lays in his arms the entire night, without Socrates succumbing to any bodily urges. Throughout the Platonic corpus, Socrates's ejaculations are only ever of the mind. Socrates can out-drink all the others; he is a terrific soldier; he is ugly as a satyr, yet is thoroughly desirable, and he can delight in the erotic without being ruled by anything other than his love of what is most important.

It is to Plato's great credit that in Pausanius's speech and character he honestly explores the relationship between eros and wisdom. Of course, the discussion is cramped culturally by the exclusively homosexual nature of the discourse and by the legalistic "solution" to the problem. The Christian response to this type of relationship is grounded in the renunciativeness which gives Christianity its power and its burden, at least when men and women, who are still animated by earthly desires try to emulate Jesus.

The power of Pausanius's speech lays in its protection of the vulnerable, but the weakness stems from the fact that what really is outside of the law is contained by the law. The trade-off between beauty and wisdom/power/wealth, particularly between young boys (and girls/women) and older men is one that can be abusive in all manner of ways, but it is one that keeps persisting to the fury and horror of the moralizing conscience. As in all these complex areas of life, love irrupts and refuses its confines. The outsider, whether the judge, the jurist, the moralist, the outraged member of the public, as with all voyeurs focus upon the sexual side. To a large, but not complete, extent, even rightly so—for this is the area where the sexual predator works, where there is no beloved, and no "purity" of heart of the seducer. However, that the predator may actually be a truly important teacher about life is something we do not want to face, because it forces us to confront the virtues that are activated in response to evil, and which may never be activated unless evil forces us to dig deep into our resources—this is something we nearly all want to refuse to countenance. But even more importantly, nothing shows us who we really are like evil. Laclos's *Dangerous Liaisons* brings this out brilliantly: for all their cunning and harm, Valmont and Madame de Merteuil show Danceny, Cecile de Volanges, and Madam de Tourvel the truth of who they really are by having them act upon what they really want.

This notwithstanding, law, like morality, wants to stop many of our real wants—law threatens force against one who would drag into the pain of evil (or at least those pains that come under its jurisdiction). Law too has a job to do in teaching him or her who spreads (certain kinds of) evil. But where there is no evil, where there is the exchange of powers that is enriching for both—a real possibility that the moralist will not countenance, but which is no less real for that—where there is the upbuildingness of love, such intrusions are themselves the pulsations of evil. In almost all areas of life there are not clear lines of good and evil. Ethics is a pale remnant of divine command, which is always universal in its commandment to love, but singular in the means of enactment. And Pausanius has touched one of great psychological complexity. Any reader of almost anything by Phillip Roth, Francine Prose's *The Blue Angel*, or Jonathon Franzen's *The Corrections* can see how the attempt to simply police that zone in which there is the passing on of the truths that only age and experience bring to youth, with all its beauty and that promise that comes from inexperience, is itself entrapped in its own potential and all too actual evils. How could it not be thus? The question of where people have the sacred right and where not to veil themselves is no easy matter anywhere, and the simple invocation, so widespread today, of the rule of equality is simply untrue, for as the social theorist Gillian Rose wrote in a beautiful and poignant book, *Love's Work*: "There is no democracy in any love relation: only mercy" and "Love in the submission of power."[11]

But Plato's Pausanius is blazing a path for deveiling that fits the more pathological side of Platonism which wants to deal with the complexity of our nature by the swift rule. His call for a legal means for handling the trade between knowledge and eros is of a piece with Plato's rule to assess whether poetry can be retained. Always and everywhere the Platonic dialogue appeals to the lawmaker(s), the wise one or few. Of course, the complexities of life, including the opportunity costs involved in time spent on coming up with rules for one range of actions as opposed to another mean that it is inevitable that decisions have to be made where there is potential violence, or widespread perceived harm. But the privilege that is bestowed when a particular point of view has the imprimatur of law means that it is very hard to overcome. This is why a culture that emphasizes openness of dialogue, something which is the most beautiful component of the Platonic dialogues generally—and, it must be said, that is most beautifully represented in Plato's most beautiful dialogue, his dialogue on beauty—is always more wise than one which judges on the basis of rules. Only by being attuned to the voices of each other can we move through the complexities of life, which love throws at us and which we are always tempted to respond to with evil. And, to repeat, nowhere is safe from this process, from this trial. And it is not simply that there is some moral code somewhere where the good are able to glow in their inner goodness. But our failures become living hells for others who are our sons, daughters, neighbors, and always our potential friends/lovers or enemies.

I have dwelt at length on the issue of eros and instruction raised by Pausanius because our age seems to have become obsessed with sexual "transgressions"—and most bewildering of all is that the institution which most valorizes "transgression" is also the most puritan and unforgiving in its desire to use the law as a "moral weapon"[12] to ensure eros does not blur institutional boundaries and social roles, and allow them to be compromised by the tumult of heart and flesh.

But where there is love between people, any transgression is a transgression against something less than love. Sexual relations are, as Lacan never ceases to say, not relations: a relation involves love. How the love between people is expressed is something that only those involved in the relationship can know. This obviously is on very dangerous ground, when the age difference is such that the younger party is a child. What constitutes a child has, like everything else in our world, been a matter of the contestations and evolution of our understanding, which eventually find enshrinement in the law. We know that it is only in rather recent times that someone capable of fathering or bearing a child is usually still considered a child, although the consensus is far from universal today. Ayatollah Khomeini, for example, made it legal for a nine-year-old girl to be marriageable (and hence sexually available to her husband) if she was fertile. (His reasoning for this has to do with the age at which Mohammad first had intercourse with his child bride Aisha—he married her when she was six.)

The classification of the child has undoubtedly some very desirable social and protective benefits—to have the young simply be sexual playthings is terrible because the zone of sexuality is so charged with other powers, as the very possibility of procreation shows all too obviously. It is also true that where there is love, the light of the intellect must come into play and not just the immediate satisfaction. The simple surrendering to the immediate as Bataille and Sade et al. want—while an understandable bodily reaction to the tyranny of rules and civilization's sacrificial requirements—is a recipe for the spread of evil because it is indifferent to everything but its own immediate enjoyment. Love's power is enhanced through its inclusion, its knowledge—the range and depth of its mediations. The very wall of social pressure, for example, that surrounds the child's sexuality is a major factor in why a loving adult should draw back from sexual congress with the young. For love demands its expansion, not the immediate satisfaction of one's desires or even just the lover's. This is a key insight of *Romeo and Juliette*, an insight which modern films of that play invariably ignore completely. This is also the truth behind the renunciative moment of love's expansion, a moment that becomes a nightmare when it is hypostasized and is used to force love into its mould. It is a truth which the nineteenth-century philosopher and historian Giuseppe Ferrari encapsulated in the formulation, and which Rosenstock-Huessy revived: "Love is desire and sacrifice in the balance."

Of the three accounts from Plato's *Symposium* that I have already mentioned, one can see that Plato has provided a youthful perspective (Phaedrus's), an elder perspective (Pausanius's), and a harmonic perspective (Eryximachus's). They are all serious perspectives. Interestingly the perspective on love that Plato expresses which has the greatest currency among the moderns is presented as a comic one—the perspective of romantic love. The comic poet Aristophanes describes the original creation of three races: the male/the female/and the hermaphrodite, each being was globular possessing four arms and four legs and "two faces, both the same, on a cylindrical neck, and one head, with one face one side and one the other, and four ears, and two lots of privates, and all other parts to match." These cartwheeling descendants of the sun (the males), the earth (females), and moon (the hermaphrodites) were arrogant enough to try and scale the heavens and take to the gods, but Zeus decided to weaken them by cleaving them asunder and remodeling them so that males and females could procreate and continue the race, while male homosexuals could obtain their desired satisfaction and then turn their attention to the everyday affairs of life (*Symposium* 191). The erotic drive which can be subdivided into heterosexual and same-sex love is not just about pleasure though. It is about the desire for union with some original part of the self. Aristophanes's speech, as comic as it is, makes the serious observation that erotic love is driven not just by the search for pleasure, but by the search for wholeness, and that in ourselves we are only a part because we are apart; we feel split from something/somebody that is essential to who we are. What Aristophanes expresses is the idea expressed in countless clichés and love songs that you and I belong together, that together we are one, that without you I am nothing, or only half, that you complete me, that you are my other half, that you are the one for me, that you are my soul mate, that you are everything I need, and hence your departure breaks me in two, leaves me empty, etc. From the Platonic position this desire for union is but a pale reflection of a deeper desire for union, the union that is achieved by the soul's recognition and achievement of its own immortality and its gaze upon the good.

The word comic, of course, does not only refer to the humorous, but also, as is evident in Dante's use of the word or in the classification of Shakespeare's *Tempest* as a comedy, the reconciling of discordances. In this sense Aristophanes describes the comic view of romantic love, the view which in Hollywood has a simple formula—does the mouse get the cheese? Yes!! Hooray. At last, they both realize that they belong together—and will always belong together. What happens after that run through the rain, or the airport, when he says for the umpteenth time, but this time with a wash of musically supported sincerity (invariably to applauding onlookers), "I love you; I can't live without you"—what happens after that does not count because wholeness has been achieved. We (should) walk out feeling, ah yes there is a bit more completeness in the world and that leaves us feeling good. The kind of harmony that Eryximachus describes in musical terms is something we feel when we achieve the kind of reconciliation with that other who is intrinsic to our very self. While Plato is aware of lovers who think this way, such love is ultimately ridiculous. To take this myth as the basis of our social reproduction and to have made of it the last myth upon which love's durability stands would have left Plato utterly bewildered and no doubt convinced of how far we had deviated from the love of wisdom which he had hoped to make the foundation of social order.

Of the positions of love outlined by Plato in the *Symposium*, the one that he sees as a genuine social threat is that advanced by the member of that group whom Plato had placed with the sophists and orators as the curse of Greek society—it is the position outlined by the tragic playwright Agathon, who, as we learn in the opening of the dialogue, has just won the annual drama prize. In other words, it is a position advanced by one whose social standing is such that what he says is taken seriously, and hence, if wrong, will have drastic social consequences. Of all the speeches in the *Symposium*, it is Agathon's alone that Socrates will rebuke, censuring it for flattering rather than praising love, for being too rhetorical in the vein of Gorgias.

Agathon says that Love is the most blessed of gods, that he is the youngest of gods, that he shuns senility, and that he loves beauty and detests ugliness. He is delicate and never injures or is injured. He is the god that brings concordance and bestows the greatest gifts on mankind. The terrible genealogy of the gods that Hesiod describes is due to Necessity not Love. And, says Agathon, had Love been "among them then, they would neither have fettered nor gelded one another; they would have used no violence at all, but lived together in peace and concord as they do today, and as they have done since Love became their heavenly Overlord" (*Symposium* 195c). Love, in tones anticipating Paul to the Corinthians, does not work by force or violence. He controls lusts and pleasures and is temperance itself, "war does not capture love, but love captures war." "Love banishes estrangement/ ushers friendship in." In addition to being the great bestower of temperance and peace, Love is a poet. "The creative power by which all living things are begotten and brought forth" he says, "is the genius of love" (197a).

Having made love the center of the pantheon, Agathon suggests (and this view is supported by all the speakers) that the intellectual contemporaries of Plato not only had a hunger for love, but also a deep dissatisfaction with the traditional pantheon. It is not Zeus, the God of the sky who dispenses good and evil and takes many forms so that he protects the earth and the hearth, property, the rights of strangers, gives laws, etc., but Love who conquers all. That is the essence of Agathon's speech. From the Platonic position, Agathon's ideas of love are too much. If right, there would be no need for reason to rule the passions, and we could achieve our greatest purposes without knowledge, let alone philosophy. Agathon's speech suggests that some of the hunger that drove the Christians also was alive in Plato's Athens. Yet Agathon's emphasis upon beauty and youth keep the belief in the power of love in a form that limits it in a way that preserves the Apollonian aspects of Greek culture.

After Agathon, Plato must clear up this danger which would make philosophy redundant. And hence Socrates's speech begins with a refutation and interrogation of Agathon, that results in that all too familiar admission of most of Socrates's interlocutors—that he did not know what he was talking about. Unlike Agathon, Socrates focuses on the lack that he gets Agathon to agree is intrinsic to love. Love longs for what it does not have. Focusing upon beauty as the end of love, he is able to reach the conclusion that love must lack beauty and thus not be the beautiful. After having given Agathon a good clip around the ear and putting him in his place, Socrates tells the party of the lessons he learnt from Diotima "a woman who was deeply versed in this and other forms of knowledge."

Diotima points out that love comes between beauty and ugliness and she denies that love is a god. The denial is based upon the Socratic/Platonic theology which radically transforms the Greek poetic conception of divinity. In the *Republic*, Plato had insisted that the poetic depiction of the gods as conniving, lustful, tricky, wheelers and dealers was a disgrace, and that the gods are simple, stable, eternal, constant in form and good—ideas and the moving stars, not the human-like Olympians, are the new gods of Platonism. In keeping with this theology, Diotima (in thoroughly Platonic defiance of anything Homeric or Hesiodic) claims that all gods are happy and beautiful, and that if there is a need, there is a degree of incompleteness that is not worthy of a divinity. Love is said to be half way between the mortal and the immortal. Love is a very powerful spirit. Rather than being a god, it is the son of Resource and Need. Love is said to be needy, barefoot, and homeless, but gallant and resourceful, and energetic. Love wants something; the gods lack nothing: they are not seekers after truth; they have it already. It is not, of course, the recognition of lack that is peculiar to Platonism and its epigoni (which, to repeat, rarely recognize their ancestry, and hence the logical implications of their choices and commitments). What is central to Platonism is that what is sought for is an idea, is something that the intellect can see and which can then form the basis for remodeling this life. The breadth of the end is such that Platonism gives the illusion that any way of thinking about the world and any way of being in the world can be grasped in Platonic terms, and hence defined and continually redefined to clarify to one's interlocutor what is going on. The knowledge of the craftsman who knows precisely what he is doing is the model which Platonism continually reproduces.

This is a fundamental error at the heart of Plato's thinking, which is perhaps most easily refuted through consideration of metaphor or art: a metaphor or work of art which can be exhaustively or completely restated into a purely denotative vocabulary or, in the case of art, into another form is ipso facto a poor metaphor or work of art. It is precisely the potency of the volatile configurations of the elements refusing to succumb to a stable order that activate our imagination and feelings at different times in different ways, sometimes to different intensities, that is peculiar to good art. Bad art with a message is merely propaganda, and Plato (and all Platonist derivatives) conceive of art as a copy of reality which is better expressed in another form, and deployed for instrumental, i.e., pedagogical purposes for those lacking the wherewithal to grasp the concepts in themselves. Good art eludes even its creator who may well commit him or herself to all sorts of formal constraints, but if those constraints lead to total artistic control, it necessarily lacks the volatility which is able to reactivate the work across the times and even within the one soul. The Platonic understanding of mimesis misses the real mimetic character of art because of the weight it places upon knowledge and consciousness. The genuinely mimetic aspect of art lies in its ability to absorb the endless interplays and triggerings of form and meaning, which precede as well as are displayed within consciousness, and which are as much a part of us, whether in waking or dream state, as of the world, whose proliferateness is as inexhaustible as our dreams and imaginings.

The artistic orientation to the world has no closure, other than an artificial one, in the beginning and end or external border. But inside the work one may move forever. And this lack of closure would suggest that the cosmos itself is infinite play in which event and purpose continually coincide. Whatever end is reached is also but a new beginning, and this process weaves on and on and in and out, as life triumphs over death, as death comes back, as the comic and the tragic continually merge into each other, and we are now present at a birth, a birthday, a funeral and on it goes. Once upon a time and happily ever after are the arbitrary closures of storytellers who know there is no closure, just a diving in somewhere and a full stop when it feels right, but the full stop is simply a caesura, a pause as we and life retake our breath, and story weaves into story and each storyteller seeks a witness to what he or she wants, or better, feels compelled, to tell. The Socratic questioning which forces the brake upon the flow of narrative is a way of enabling us to take some control of the reality of which we are part.

This is undoubtedly a greatness of Platonic philosophy—even if that greatness is purchased by excessive claims about reason's merits, and capacities.

The closure of Platonism is when the soul returns to its home, a grander closure than mere knowledge, but the Platonic picture of reality can be seen as a series of concentric circles of cosmos, city, and soul, in which each has its own harmony—the first imposed by a demiurge who sees the form of the good, the second by the philosopher king/legislator who knows and rules by the idea of the good and the third the philosopher who teaches others about the idea of the good. Wisdom is required everywhere, no less by the creator god, who has it, and the philosopher who seeks it. And the Platonic doctrine of love in the *Symposium* gets off the ground at that moment when Love is said to be a lover of wisdom. And a party which began with the theme of praising the neglected god of love begins to reach its high point with the dedivinization of the former god, as the love of wisdom in the pursuit of the nature of love takes over the traditional way of speaking about love. The reworking of a culture's vocabulary, which is the undertaking of every great philosophy, and which, as we have suggested, in Plato's case requires a thorough overhaul of what constitutes the divine powers, does not take its bearing from Love, but from wisdom. To say it again, in the Socratic love of wisdom, the Platonic emphasis is upon the wisdom that is loved; the love is not an end state but the propellant force which pushes us to the end of the good and the virtues which exhibit goodness, the chief of which is wisdom.

On this basis, love is redefined as "renowned and all-beguiling power [which] includes every kind of longing for happiness and the good" (205d). It is not, as Aristophanes earlier claimed, the search for the other half, but the search for the good. "Love never longs for anything but the good, and love longs for the good to be his own forever." Of course, from the Platonic position Aristophanes's story of the search for the other half is a search for something that we believe to be good. And the Platonic move is the insistence that this essence exists, that the pleasurable, the noble self-sacrifice, the harmony, the romantic comedy is desired by us because we want the good, and these states and activities are but the residual aspects, the shimmering husks of the essence which the mind itself can comprehend, appreciate, and be elevated by. The restlessness of our existence which drives us from one activity to another is but the indication of our desire for rest, just as the plethora of good things which we seek nourishment from is the sign of our desire for the good itself. Stability, eternity, and idea or form, a place to rest, that is what Plato believes we are all really seeking. Love is a symptom of our restlessness. To be sure it is that intermediary between immortality and mortality which is the bridge leading us beyond ourself. The transcendence that in one way or another is expressed in each of the speeches, is represented within a metaphysical context that for the Platonist, enables the poetic aspiration to take on the more secure footing of philosophical truth.

The Platonic steps are that "to love is to bring forth upon the beautiful, both in body and in soul," that "love is not the longing for the beautiful, but for the conception and generation that the beautiful effects" and that "love is longing for immortality." For Plato, "the mortal does all it can to put on immortality." And he brilliantly connects how we pursue immortality in our natural activities as in our institutions. By breeding, he says, "we ensure that there will always be a younger generation to take the place of the old?" "Procreation is how the temporal partakes of the eternal." Man's greatest incentive is the love of glory, and men are driven "to win eternal mention in the deathless roll of fame" (208c). "Everyone of us, no matter what he does is longing for the endless fame, the incomparable glory that is theirs, and the nobler he is, the greater his ambition, because he is in love with the eternal." At its most basic level this longing for immortality can be found in "those whose procreativity of the body turn to woman as the object of their love, and raise a family, in the blessed hope that by doing so they will keep their memory green, through time and through eternity." And just as there is the procreativity of nature and the body, there is procreativity of the spirit exemplified through poets and lawgivers.

Love is an ascendant force, and beauty is the power that draws the lover forward and assists in the ascension. The ascension is depicted by Plato as being from love of one beauty in one body to love of beauty in beautiful bodies in general. This in turn leads to love of beauty of the soul which is higher than love of beauty of bodies. The love of spiritual beauty also has its ascension. The love of beauty of laws and institutions leads to love of beauty of the sciences and every kind of knowledge and love of beauty in itself leads to perfect virtue. The immortality of the soul and the perpetuity of what is best and noblest, this is the grandeur of the Platonic vision. Whether it can be achieved with the Platonic means, whether reason is up to the task is the question, just as it is questionable whether the good is stable and eternal, whether the good is what Plato wants it to be—that is what that other great current that flows from love in our tradition makes us consider if we understand it. Its orientation to reality and hence its conception of love has nothing to do with argument, or with the competitive poetics which mark the *Symposium*. Unlike the New Testament, the *Symposium* carries neither urgency nor desperation in its conception of love. It is as timeless in its presentation of what lovers of truth and a drink are capable of as is its central message about the purpose of love and beauty. Even more than the *Republic*, the *Symposium* represents the Platonic ideal of what people are capable of, and the payoff of philosophy—it is a delight to be among friends and to praise love and to try and grasp its essence and to engage in argument and to contemplate our perpetuity in our children, in our name becoming famous, in our institutions and laws and in our very own soul. Socrates will be martyred and Alcibiades will die horribly, but they are immortalized in their laughter in that little oasis, in that imagined eternity of the drinking party. The Platonic view of love is lovely and joyful, but it is unreal in that it is but a momentary escape. There is wine at the last supper, but what to the Greeks is a symbol of joy becomes a sign of blood, of the blood that is needed for joy's final triumph—a triumph only reached after the great suffering of the crucifixion. There is, of course, much mention of joy in the New Testament, but little of laughter, even if the news is good.

All gospels lead to the crucifixion and all epistles lead from it. The desperateness of the human condition and the absolute importance of the crucifixion is nowhere better formulated than in Paul's *Letter to the Romans* (8:22) "for we know that the whole creation groans and travails in pain together until now." The greatness of the pain that requires that we think of the entirety of creation gives us some idea of the desperation of the search for a way out that informs the Christian conception of love. Plato tells us profound things about love, but there is more to tell and the telling is different when it comes from men who were driven by the utmost despair to create a new future. To be sure, there is despair in Plato, despair about the city states tearing themselves apart, and by the time of Aristotle they are all but a spent force politically. And Plato believes that were we but philosophical enough, this would cease. But the accumulated generational despair of the Jews had no faith in a solution being provided by ideas and eternal stabilities such as the good. Tenaciously, the Jewish people held on to the promise of God's love. The Christians announced, as folly to Greeks and as sacrilege to Jews, that God's love now walked among them and that His love came in the form of the sacrifice of Himself in the form of His Son.

Notes

1.   See Harold Berman's masterly *Law and Revolution: The Formation of the Western Legal Tradition*, (Cambridge, MA: Harvard University Press, 1983).

2.   See G. W. F. Hegel, *Hegel's Logic: Being Part One of the Encyclopaedia of the Philosophical Sciences (1830) (Hegel's Encyclopedia of the Philosophical Sciences)*, trans. J. F. Findlay and William Wallace, (Oxford: Oxford University Press, 1975), "Introduction," sec. 7.

3.   Geoffrey Grigson, *The Goddess of Love: The Birth, Triumph, Death and Return of Aphrodite* (London: Constable, 1976), 19.

4.   Bernard Knox, *"Introduction" to Homer's Iliad*, trans. Robert Fagles (New York: Viking/Penguin, 1990), 45. Translations from the *Iliad* are from this edition.

5.   All references to Plato will follow the standard practice of including references in brackets which refer to the Stephanus edition, invariably included in the margins of English translations. All translations of Plato are from *The Collected Dialogues of Plato*, ed. Edith Hamilton and Huntington Cairns (Princeton, NJ: Princeton University Press, 1961).

6.   Of the vast literature on the *Gorgias*, I must recommend the brilliantly insightful *Socrates in the Underworld: On Plato's Gorgias* by Nalin Ranasinghe (Indiana: St. Augustine's Press, 2009).

7.   *Theages 125e–126a* in Mark Joyal, *The Platonic Theages: An Introduction*, Commentary and Critical ed. (Stuttgart: Franz Steiner Verlag, 2000), 149.

8.   Joyal, *Platonic Theages*, 149.

9.   Rosenstock-Huessy, *Lectures on Comparative Religion-1954*, vol. 8— Lecture 17, November 18, 1954, available on *The Collected Works of Eugen Rosenstock-Huessy* on DVD (Norwich, VT: Argo Books, 2005).

10.   In book 2, chapters 2 and 3 of *Things Hidden since the Foundation of the World*, Girard argues against any sacrificial reading of the gospels and scripture. Girard, though, is really arguing against the idea that God wants a sacrifice, that God encourages the mimetic contagion and that His way out of violence is the mythical way of the "sacrifice." I agree entirely with this, but what Girard does not adequately distinguish here is the difference between making the Other the sacrifice, and God Himself being the sacrifice in order to bring this process to an end by showing it for what it is—viz. murder. Later he will be more precise, distinguishing between, "sacrifice of the other, self-sacrifice, and Christian sacrifice." *Battling to the End: Conversations with Benoît Chantre*, trans. Mary Baker (East Lansing: Michigan State University Press, 2010), 35. Christian sacrifice is accurately and succinctly expressed by Robert Hamerton-Kelly: "Christ is a divine offering to humankind, not a human offering to God." *Sacred Violence: Paul's Hermeneutic of the Cross* (Minneapolis, MN: Fortress, 1992), 80. By Jesus being willing to be the sacrifice (and in the case of Plato's *Apology*, Socrates accepts his sacrificial destiny), he does not condone the cross, i.e., he does not wish for others to crucify. But he makes of it something that is stronger than death, and thus he, as victim,

potentially redeems the future victim by showing the victimizer the sin of his act.

11.   Gillian Rose and Michael Wood, *Love's Work* (New York: Vintage, 1997), 55.

12.   I thank my friend and colleague Chris Hutton for the felicitous formulation.

2

The Love of Christ

From the church a fellowship was created which crossed social, tribal, ethnic, and later national boundaries. No student of European history can fail to note its presence, even if there is no shortage of historians who are baffled or disgusted by it. The sacrament of communion which made humans become one with the body of Christ was equally a means of making human beings one with each other—the sacramental act symbolizing the unity of the double injunction at the core of the Christian religion—love the lord thy God with all thy heart and love thy neighbor as thyself. The fact that Christians could still be enemies—that men and women remained shaped by other forces, particularly those involving different political interests—indicates that what is astonishing is how the church managed to build a relatively unified body. Of course, there were schisms, and major severances such as the split between the Roman and the Orthodox churches of the East, as well as wars against heretical sects. But the church provided western Europe, at least up until the Reformation, with a spiritual unanimity of purpose that it had never experienced before, even under the military might of the Romans.

As important as philosophy is to the West, the very incorporation of philosophy into the West suggests that its potency was subordinate to a more potent institutional power than itself. For philosophy of itself could become a powerful force only once, a degree of unity it never managed to achieve was already in existence. Ancient philosophers dreamt of unity, but such unity was limited—to dreaming. Plato, for example, urged Greeks to see each other as one, but not by becoming an imperial power of the sort that the Macedonian Alexander established. And Cicero armed with his belief in natural law spoke beautifully of men in all places and at all times possessing the one reason and hence being subject to the one law, regardless of where or when they lived. But that idea belonged to a man who would be embroiled in the turmoil of Rome's civil wars and leadership life and death struggles which were as remote from natural law as it was possible to be. The Stoics too had spoken of a universal brotherhood, and among their kind they could include a slave (Epictetus) and an emperor (Marcus Aurelius), and while the latter may well have been a good man and left a legacy of powerful maxims, he was unable to solve one of the most important problems of politics—that of succession. And the empire was, as Dio Cassius put it, to turn from "a kingdom of gold to one of iron and rust" thanks to his son Commodus.

Be that as it may, ancient philosophy never forged a unity in any way comparable to what the church actually did. It was the church that provided a unity as the Roman imperium fragmented (though it could be argued, as Gibbon did, that the church is a major factor in the decline of the Roman Empire in the first place). To be sure, the church quickly incorporated philosophy, though some of its earliest thinkers such as Tertullian and Tatian were hostile to philosophy as a corrupting practice, corrupting because its elevation of the mind threatened the life of faith which recognizes the limits of the mind (this is a recurrent theme in the history of Christianity, and finds powerful expression in Luther's attack upon Aristotle and his influence upon Catholicism). But once Rome's administrative system became lost and the outward signs of Rome's greatness—its roads, architecture, bathhouses, aqueducts, sewerage system, and amphitheaters—became ruins and the tendrils of nature occupied what the tribes had clamored over but not refashioned, it was the church that eventually provided sufficient cultural/spiritual unity for men of different tongues eventually even to revive the ancient institutions, the universities, throughout Europe. The university was a philosophical, more specifically, a Platonic, invention (the academy was originally the name of Plato's school outside of Athens). But the university as we know it was a Christian institution dedicated to carrying out God's work in the realms of the mind, hence the original importance of theology in the curriculum, and the role it played in preparing men for the professions of medicine and law. It was the church that provided a common tongue so that men of letters could communicate their ideas and collectively pool their knowledge. The ancient philosophical schools were fundamentally schismatic and comparatively small in scale. Their emphasis upon the primacy of intelligence always meant that its reach could never match an institution which could incorporate the common and simple folk as well as aspirants of wisdom, and which as far as judgment day was concerned treated all souls (a feast day which Rosenstock-Huessy identifies as "the first universal democracy")[1] as of one and the same, whether philosopher, emperor, pope, widow, or orphan. And finally, it was the church that provided the belief in the incremental achievements of generations as men and women cooperated in building cathedrals not to the glory of a man or a man who wanted to demonstrate his divine origin through his marshalling of earthly power, such as the Egyptians and other imperial orders, but for the glory of God and all God's souls.

The fact that both the university and churches have a contemporary presence, which is far less potent now than the forms they have spawned in a society which is predominantly secular, more obviously dedicated to the proliferation of material possibilities and commercial gain, to the pursuit of personal choices and scientific investigation/ research and development rather than spiritual growth or the pursuit of wisdom, conceals their original potency and mission. Yet, visibility is only the momentary face of a power. Reality is process, and just as the beginnings of things are always invisible, and all beginnings can be dissolved into prior processes, powers divest themselves so that they recede from the visibility of the general consciousness as new forms evolve. The immediacy, understandably enough, conceals past as much as future. And it is only when we ask about yesterday, or work (in hope and faith and love) on creating a better tomorrow that the visible immediate power takes on secondary importance. Moreover, what we wish to create and what we do create increasingly mismatches as more factors are involved. Luther no more dreamt of being a major contributor to a conception of freedom which would ultimately create the secular state than he dreamt of flying to the moon, yet the effect of Luther's efforts to free Christians from the whore of Rome was to create a space where people could be free to leave what they saw as the superstitions of Christianity behind while walking away with the belief in the fundamental equality of human beings and the right to pursue their own lifestyles so long as they did not harm others. The leap between Luther and liberal secularism is no more incongruous than the leap between Christ and his disciples and the intrigues and machinations of papal politics.

Whatever world rebuilding truth is contained in Christianity flows from its awareness of and response to love. Christianity is, of course, originally a Jewish sect which takes its direction from the Jewish command to love God and the neighbor. And as Anders Nygren rightly notes:

> As early as Hosea the principle that love is the central requirement of the Law is clearly recognized; God desires "love and not sacrifice" (Hos. vi. 6). Indeed, love towards God sometimes acquires such importance it can stand alongside "the fear of the Lord" as an inclusive description of the right attitude of man to God. There are thus to be found in Judaism definite impulses towards making the commandment of Love in this sense "the great commandment of the Law."[2]

While the commandments of Yahweh hold true for all peoples, Judaism restricts its horizon to God's elect, the children of Israel. Perhaps no thinker has done such a profound job as Franz Rosenzweig in showing how Christianity is ever dependent upon Judaism. For the Jewish faith is, he argues, built around two traits. The first is the most elemental triad of God, Human, and World. And he argues that all peoples, at least until philosophy had blinded their reasoning with its false totality of reason's all-embracing sphericality, had known that human beings, the world, and (the) God(s) refer to aspects of existence that were (in Schelling's term) "positive" existents—inescapable parts of the lifeworld of a people. But, he continued, unlike other peoples, the Jews discerned a fundamental alignment between these different grounding "elements" so that a relationship was seen as existing in which there was mutual responsiveness. Indeed, a definition of a god is that it is a living power that commands responsiveness. Thus, God was affected by a human's behavior as much as a human by God's, and the responsiveness on the part of God was, in turn, part of a greater promise. That promise, though, could only be grasped through a fundamental attunement to the voice of God, which Rosenzweig argues is discernible in the very grammar of life. And he argues that grammar is registered and given form in the Bible—thus, for him, it is the great miracle of the Bible, and the truth behind the elected nature of the Jewish peoples. For being attuned to the relationship between God, Human, and World, the Jewish people further open themselves up to another plane of reality which is constituted by another relationship—this is the overlapping triad of Creation, Revelation, and Redemption. It would take us too far afield here to track down the argument he makes about the grammar of Creation, Revelation, and Redemption—which I discuss at length in my forthcoming book, *Religion, Redemption and Revolution: The New Speech Thinking of Franz*

Rosenzweig and Eugen Rosenstock-Huessy[3]—here just let me say that he bases his argument on a grammatical analysis of *Genesis, The Song of Songs*, and *Psalm* 115. The grammar itself is what gives body to the content, and the content is nothing less than the core of the Jewish faith, that God creates the world and it is good, so good that He reveals the secret that love is as strong as death, and He wishes to redeem creation through love. Such redemption can only be achieved through we creatures loving each other enough to join in the community of love that sings the praise of love itself and the God who commands this love and who wishes for redemption. Indeed this striving for redemption, though, involves nothing less than the triple redemption of God Himself, as well as Humanity and World. For the redeemed, World is the World charged completely by God's love—freed of the hatred and evil and the damnable. For Rosenzweig, the Jews were not only the people who first heard, recorded, and attended to this command to *love* their God, but their very existence is built around this commandment and the subsequent anticipation of redemption, which is God's promise. That anticipation is their very dwelling, and that dwelling is not so much a "belief" but a way of being ensconced in their liturgy, festivals, and rituals. The Jews are, for Rosenzweig, the "coals in the eternal fire" of God. Being thus does not mean that their life is all floss and candy—far from it, it means living in the suffering of the distance between God's promised future redemption and the unredeemed present, unredeemed because human hearts continue in their own blind selfish desire—with all its mimesis, folly, and acquisitiveness.[4] But that very suffering is redeemable insofar as it is God's love that is being suffered for and toward which it contributes to the expansiveness that is redemption.

Rosenzweig had come to realize the full extent of his Jewishness only through the near conversion experience he had in 1913 through his conversations with his friend, Eugen Rosenstock-Huessy, and his cousins Rudi and Hans Ehrenberg (all three were Jewish apostates who converted to Christianity). But he came to see that the Christian needs the Son to reach the Father, while the Jews have always been with the father and thus need no mediator. His masterpiece *The Star of Redemption*, has been appreciated by Christians as well as Jews, in part because of how it teaches the common core of the Jewish and Christian faiths. For Rosenzweig, the being of the Jews is a being through blood, not through allegiance to ideas. Given that the National Socialists would base their anti-Semitic policies and acts precisely on the basis of Jewishness being racial rather than religious, *The Star* is an extraordinary prophetic work calling upon Jews to acknowledge their being while pleading with Christians to appreciate their own dependency upon the revelatory truth and necessity for the continued existence of the Jewish people.

What Rosenzweig appreciated and accentuated in his work was that the task of Christianity was to universalize the revelatory and redemptive truth of God's command to love. Thus, did the truth that was revealed to the Jewish people expand within the pagan world—but, he noted, always prone to the danger that the pagan side of Christianity would ever struggle with its Jewish center, and that the struggle would inevitably time and time again reduce Christianity to just another pagan coalition of forces, at least until, once again, its inner command be heard again and the fire of God's love enflame Christian souls to once more hearken to the mission of redemption. Rosenzweig's observations regarding the perennial pagan temptations of Christianity are a brilliant insight into why the Christian world constantly lapses into its opposite. Where Rosenzweig is less convincing, and less critical, is on the question of Judaism's failures. To be sure, his brief was shaped by an environment in which liberalized Jews had lost touch with what he saw as the true meaning of their heritage and in which Christians were being drawn yet again into a pagan maw. While paganism is capable of many shapes, he saw, like few around him, that in the immediate aftermath of the Great War, and in the abdication of the Kaiser, the new democracy would be fueled by, and in turn fuel, the fires of anti-Semitism. Furthermore, Rosenzweig saw that anti-Jewishness, a Christian pathology based upon resentment of the stubborn refusal of the Jews to join them, could not simply be equated with anti-Semitism, a pseudorace-based science which wanted to ensure that Jews could never join them. To be sure anti-Jewishness frequently exploded into violence, and it was often a conductor for mob violence. Christians who are caught up in the violent mimetic contagion are no less enflamed than anyone else. Being Christian, in the sense of following Christ, means to refuse to feed the contagion, to stop it going further, even at the price of being a martyr so that a link in the chain is broken. Anti-Semitism can never be Christian because it violates the core law of the Christian faith—the law of love. Rosenzweig saw that anti-Jewishness may be driven by the law of love—for it wants to share the good news, and to embrace the person who it believes needs to enter into the higher faith. But, the history of anti-Jewishness shows that the slippage from love to fanaticism is so frequent that it might well be inevitable. Moreover, Rosenzweig provided such a powerful argument for the meaning of the Jews that since him, at least, it is hard to conceive of a rejoinder—and he convinced his close friends and cousins who had converted to Christianity that he had made the right choice. And thus did Hans Ehrenberg argue that there was only one permissible way in which a Christian might convert a Jew—not through argument, but through the example of his or her own life.

And while there was no shortage of German pastors and priests ready to substitute Hitler for Christ, and the Germans for God's children, such a substitution was no more intrinsic to the teaching of Christianity than any lie or counterfeit is the intrinsic meaning of any truth. This is not to deny that Christians and Jews were and ultimately still are inimical. Again this was well appreciated by Rosenzweig, who, in the dialogue conducted with Rosenstock-Huessy, realized (as did Rosenstock-Huessy) that the victory of their dialogue was not in the denial of mutual enmity, but in their willingness to serve on a common front in spite of their inimical faiths. I underscore this in order to accentuate the fact that while Christianity, as Rosenzweig, rightly argues is dependent upon Judaism, and in some fundamental ways finds itself expressing the core of the Jewish faith—love of God and love of the neighbor—the dispute between the two faiths emerges out of a perceived failure of Judaism originally by Jews themselves.

That the earliest Christians draw upon the resources of the Old Testament to establish the New Testament is indicative of their belief in the necessity of continuity between their own endeavors and that of the history and God of their forefathers; but that they also believed that the Jewish faith had run into a dead end, that it blinded its followers and made them as complicit in the evils of the world as the other peoples of the world. The Jews, for the followers of Jesus, were no longer elect, but their election was the phantasm in which they enshrouded themselves in order to continue their godless conduct. But before we look more closely at this rift which originally takes place in Judaism, let us look more closely at the idea of love in Christianity and its overlaps and emphases in comparison with Judaism and the Greeks.

Judaism and Christianity introduce a component of love so fundamental to their purposes and yet different to Greek conceptions that, at least in its earliest Greek/Christian articulations, it requires a new designation, that of agape. And agape is invariably contrasted with eros, the love that Plato explores in the *Phaedrus* and *Symposium*.

Irving Singer puts it succinctly when he writes: "Eros was merely the spirit of movement within the world. But agape is the Holy Spirit, the spirit of God himself, active in the world and yet belonging to another realm."[5] Other Greek words for love are also used in the New Testament—*philia* or *phileo* (fellowship and community) usually translated as fellowship and *storge* (familial love). Moreover, the word agape is not invented by the Christians, it has a classical pedigree (though it was not a common word in literature) and within its original semantic field it no way indicates a sharp conceptual difference from eros. Yet, as it has often been pointed out, the New Testament does not contain the word eros (it is in the *Septuagint*, the Greek version of the Old Testament in Proverbs 7:18, where a prostitute says "Come, let us take our fill of love until morning; let us solace ourselves with love"), thus indicating that eros represented something fundamentally different to what the writers of the New Testament wished to capture when they spoke of love. At the heart of the matter is the sensuousness that the term eros alludes to that Plato draws upon even though he teaches that eros lifts us beyond the senses. On the other hand, as William Phipps pointed out in "The Sensuousness of *Agape*," agape is used in the Septuagint Old Testament where agape manifestly has a sensuous dimension.[6]

The writer whose examination of agape and eros has had the greatest impact is Anders Nygren. He has stressed the outward, downward flowing, irrational, selfless, (self-)sacrificial, unmotivated character of agape in contrast to the self-assertive, acquisitive, motivated, striving, upward, willful, ultimately ego and human-centric character of eros. For Nygren, the fundamental difference between the two modes of love is also encapsulated in the end states (often enough confused but fundamentally different in conception and religious significance) that each leads toward immortality of the soul (eros) and resurrection (agape). While Nygren does an excellent job of illuminating much of the peculiarly Christian component of love, his accentuation of the distinction between agape and eros, as Singer and others have noticed, means that almost no one apart from him, Marcion, and Luther have gasped the central teaching of Christian love. Singer also rightly makes the point that Nygren's treatment of Luther is one that overlooks the temporal forces which are so important for understanding Luther's own theological emphasis.[7] That is, in both its intellectual and non-temporal emphases, Nygren himself misses something of fundamental importance. It is this omission that leads him to take an important

Christian contribution to the character of love, as if that contribution meant the outright rejection of all that had previously been realized about love. The potency of Christianity does indeed lie in its expansion of the meaning of God's love and human love for God, but the emphasis upon self-sacrifice and surrender to God does not altogether eliminate the motivation and striving and willful components of human experience. That is, in overemphasizing the uniqueness of the Christian comprehension of love, he underplays how the Christian teaching of love taps into the love already fathomed by Greeks and Jews, not to mention others. Moreover, the subsequent absorption of Greek philosophy into Christian thought facilitates a further revelation about the power of love that only fully manifests because of that absorption. None of this is to say that there is not something important in the distinction between agape and eros, just that the differences do not require the kind of excision suggested by Nygren. Nor does this mean that there is not something fundamentally revolutionary about the Christian way of seeing life—a revolution as we have hinted at above that takes its point of departure from Judaism and the crisis within Judaism.

Nevertheless, there is no equivalent to Plato's starting point of erotic desire for achieving immortality in the New Testament. However, it can be argued that insofar as *The Song of Songs* is an integral part of the revelation of God's word, it along with such commendations of love between husband and wife as in *Ecclesiastes* (9:9), or Jacob's love for Rachel suggests that the earliest Christians, like the Jews, acknowledged that there is a legitimate sphere in which erotic desire receives divine sanction. The common allegorical interpretation of *The Song of Songs* also indicates how the Christian tradition may see erotic desire, in terms similar to Plato, as finding genuine fulfillment in the union with the divine (though, it is more likely that this only testifies to the fact that Platonism took root within the church and hence those sprung from its branches saw their teachings sprouting everywhere throughout the Bible).

Unlike the Old Testament, the New Testament never focuses upon the positive aspects of erotic desire. Sexual congress is sanctified within marriage, but as Jesus's life exemplifies and Paul stipulates, the Christian preference is for a life of sexual abstinence, although this will not be achievable by the majority. In this respect, it is vastly different in its emphasis than what we find in the modern industrialized world with its preoccupation with sex and desire. It is also vastly different from the homoeroticism that is littered throughout Plato's corpus. Generally, the New Testament's engagement with erotic desire is in the proscriptions of transgressive behaviors, in particular lewdness, lust, covetousness, incest, adultery, and homosexuality.[8] Its emphasis upon the spiritual dangers of erotic desire is largely continuous with the Jewish emphases of the Old Testament (from Adam's succumbing to Eve to David's desire for Bathsheba). The New Testament has often been seen as somehow depicting a softer less vengeful God; some like Marcion, for example, claimed that the New Testament introduced a completely new God who overthrows the vengeful deity of the Old Testament. Lending support to such a view are passages such as John's "Fear is not in love, but perfect love casteth out fear; because fear hath torment. He that feareth is not made perfect in love" (1 John 4:18). Leaving aside for now the issue of fear and love and the respective qualities of Yahweh (a name that does not appear in the New Testament) and the Father and Lord of Christ and his disciples, it is the case that far from softening the Old Testament's emphasis upon transgression, the New Testament intensifies the ascetic elements of the Jewish tradition by making the perfect man and Son of God completely without sexual desire, and the son of a virgin. Jesus's followers like Jesus himself have no sexual life once they join him.

Jesus is also conscious of the fact that he is taking his teaching on the evils of sexual transgression to a deeper level by insisting that the inner desire is every bit as significant as outer act: "Ye have heard that it was said by them of old time, Thou shalt not commit adultery: But I say unto you, that whoever looketh on a woman to lust after her hath committed adultery already in his heart" (Matthew 5:27–28). And then the command that finds its fulfillment in Origen's act of self-castration a century and a half later: "And if thy right eye offend thee, pluck it out, and cast it from thee: for it is profitable for thee that one of thy members should perish, and not that thy whole body should be cast into hell. And if thy right hand offend thee, cut it off, and cast it from thee that one of thy members should perish, and not that thy whole body be cast into hell" (Matthew 5:29–30). If, however, such sayings are placed in the context of loving and not judging, they lose their savage asceticism and judgmentalism, and make all question their own purity. That one alone is the Son of God would suggest that we are all guilty of such sins, and we must begin with forgiving each other for we all sin in our heart. In spite of that, Paul lists in Corinthians (1. 6:9–10) those who will not inherit the kingdom of God: the fornicators, idolaters, adulterers, the effeminate or voluptuous, sodomites (*arsenokoitai*), thieves, covetous persons, drunkards, revilers, and the rapacious.[9] Thus, he who emphasizes that we must not judge, does judge, and with that he places Christianity on a clear moral footing which easily opens the gate up to a puritanical and punitive phantasmic form of faith which has so often plagued it. I do not want to imply that Jesus welcomes adultery, fornication, theft and the like, but he sees humankind as so prone to sin that the emphasis is not on judging the sin but on loving the sinner in spite of the sin and inviting the sinner into a new or higher kind of joyful life.

The New Testament represents the earliest Christians as sharing an inner calm, a joy and potency that is due to a spiritual communion, rather than an emphasis upon the asceticism of the flesh. Their renunciativeness is infinitely more liberating than onerous, and more an act of simply discarding than a great struggle—though again Paul seems to see more struggle than simple decision to choose joy over suffering, which might tell us about his temperament and about the struggles of new Christians wanting to have the joy that had been promised, but perhaps seemed to escape them. But it also must be said that the ascetic attitude to sex is part of a broader asceticism. It is not that Jesus or his followers are incapable of seeing the beauties of the earth, but they reserve their appreciation for the simple things, the "lilies of the field." Like the Epicureans, the early Christians saw that the attachments that are part and parcel of public office and the enjoyment of wealth are also part of what must be renounced in order to do the Father's will. Compared to the leisured politicized homosexuals reclining at Plato's *Symposium* while celebrating the marvels of love, and seen from a more worldly perspective, the early Christians are a humorless, troubled, and fanatical group. From the perspective of the evangelicals, the Platonists are frivolous and self-indulgent pretty boys and pedophiles insensitive to suffering who wish to give an inflated spirituality to their carnality. But it is important to keep in mind the point made by G. Rattray Taylor about Christ in *Sex in History*, that book which makes such a compelling case for seeing so much of Christianity's attitude to sex as death-driven neurosis, that:

> at no point does He advocate or practice masochism. He made one long fast in order to undergo a spiritual experience, but in general we find Him recognizing the importance of and satisfying human needs—feeding crowds, defying Jewish law to relieve His own hunger on a Sabbath, and even turning water to wine for a wedding feast.

> Nor did He anathematize sexual pleasure.... His consideration of the woman taken in adultery hardly suggests a puritanical attitude to sex.[10]

Not puritanical, for the puritanical is obsessed with what it wants to repress, thereby becoming something even worse in its treatment of its neighbor (equally as cruel but with the added mystification of sanctimony) than that of the debauched. The position of the early Christians on sexual matters was generally—and this is largely true of Paul—as Rattray Taylor rightly says, one which sought to "substitute the transcendence of sexual instincts for the technique of dealing with them by catharsis" (adding, that the church dropped "this device of sublimation for repression").[11]

As different as the paeans to love expressed in a banquet are from the love that leads to and beyond the crucifixion, there was an ascetic strain in Greek philosophy which finds itself in the behaviors of Socrates, his own simple life, and his mastery of his sexual passions (in spite of having had children). The earlier Orphic and Pythagorean traditions which Plato frequently refers to are also steeped in asceticism. It is as true of the Greek and Roman philosophers that asceticism was almost universally seen as a means for distinguishing the serious from the self-indulgent. A point strikingly brought home by the fact that the Stoics and Epicureans could dispute on all manner of things, about the virtue of public life, about the place of pleasure in the scheme of life, about the primary stuff of the cosmos, but both schools saw that the pursuit of wealth diminished the soul. Hence the Epicureans's contempt for Seneca whose material possessions were so disproportionate to the austerity preached in his writings. The same was largely true of the flourishing religious sects. There were some that taught indulgence and sexual abandon, but the hunger that cut across all class lines was too deep to be satisfied by sexuality. In sum, asceticism was a common spiritual life-choice and when St. Paul wrote the following to the Romans he was expressing what was indeed essential, but not unique, to the followers of Christ:

> they that are after the flesh do mind the things of the flesh; but that they that are after the Spirit the things of the Spirit. For to be carnally minded is death; but to be spiritually minded is life and peace. Because the carnal mind is enmity against God: for it is not subject to the law of God, neither indeed can be. So then they that are in the flesh cannot please God. (Romans 1:5–8)

Christianity was but one sect jostling for room among a throng of religious and philosophic ascetic doctrines. Indeed, the ascetic sensibility and attitude was so widespread that no religion which lacked this characteristic could have had mass appeal. To the modern mind this seems unbelievable. The view of religion expressed by Karl Marx, for example, is now almost a commonplace belief among the educated. Marx held that heaven was the creation of the oppressed who would no longer seek solace in an after-world once there was material fulfillment and human solidarity based upon common ownership on this earth. The problem with this belief is that the revulsion to the bread and circus society with its borderless sexualities and cruel theatricalities cut across all classes and peoples. Marxism may have held the hope of solving one of the causes of revulsion (the cruelty some classes inflict upon others), but the motivation behind the austerity of philosophers and religious cults was equally a sense of revulsion at self-satiation itself. The hunger for meaning in one's own personal life could no more then as now be satisfied in any way by having more or better material goods. That hunger meant reaching out and within: out to one's neighbor in order to create a new kind of community, one not based on class or nation, but a shared spirit of what one loved (hence also the growing cosmopolitanism among philosophical schools), and within to one's God. A large part of the success of Christianity lay in how far out and how far in it promised to take one. The philosophical schools of Stoicism and Epicureanism as well as most other philosophical schools, including Aristotelianism and the pre-neo-Platonist remnants of Platonism seemed to take one in as far as doctrine or a set of explanatory principles facilitating reconciliation of some sort with reality, but the experience within stopped well short of the mystic subsumption promised in the mystery schools, in the proliferating pre-Gnostic and subsequent Gnostic sects and neo-Platonic schools. Christianity had a spiritual depth, and an ascetic and ecstatic strain compatible with, indeed nourishing Gnosticism, but it had a breadth and all-inclusiveness that enabled it to outlast potential Gnostic usurpers of its own gospels. Generally, the spiritual need meant either the outgrowth of the philosophical methods or, as in neo-Platonism, a complete revamping of what philosophy was. When Lucian, in the early second century AD, ridicules the philosophers' schools with his portrait of scruffy shallow scoundrels armed with threadbare beliefs and bloated rhetoric, we have a wonderful view of what a failure philosophy had become in its ability to satiate the spiritual hunger of the times. The bemusement of Lucian at the number of sects competing for adherents, combined with his solid good sense shows the breadth of spiritual instability he saw around him. The only serious pagan philosophical spiritual alternative to the Christian and Gnostic schools to emerge in the empire was a reconstructed Platonism that based itself entirely upon the religious/mystical elements of Plato. But it was still a philosophy and hence only for the relative few. It was also too late for such a philosophy to do anything other than be channeled into the conduits allowed for it by a more triumphant Christianity. Thus, for example, in the writings of pseudo-Dionysius we see a thoroughly neo-Platonic teaching (borrowed in great slabs from Proclus) in Christian dress. Seen from the purview of the Gospels and evangelists, neo-Platonism still carries its Greek burden of wisdom which gives it a different accentuation to the more simple, but all the more effective "let your communication be, Yea, yea; Nay, nay: for whatsoever is more than these cometh of evil" (Matthew 5:37). Like all truth, though, these words in service to a spirit that is not Holy are capable of generating enormous damage.

While the evolution of Christianity is inseparable from its incorporation of Greek philosophy and the subsequent doctrinal differences and shadings that is largely, if not exclusively, due to the intellectual role played by theology, early Christianity is as distrustful of Greek wisdom in general as of philosophy in particular. In his first Epistle to the Corinthians, Paul insists that Christ crucified is a stumbling block to the Jews and foolishness to the Greeks and that God has chosen the foolish things of the world to confound the wise. Significantly, the words concept, idea, and category do not appear in the Bible. Concomitantly, the words philosophy and philosophers do not appear in the Old Testament. And the depiction of those who try to fathom the justice of God in Job unequivocally shows us why that tradition did not leave itself open to philosophy. The writers of the New Testament inhabited a world where philosophy's presence had established itself, yet it is only mentioned twice: in Colossians 2:8 where Paul says "See to it that no one takes you captive through hollow and deceptive philosophy, which depends on human tradition and the basic principles of this world rather than on Christ," and in Acts (17:18) where Paul encounters Stoics and Epicureans, some of whom see him as a "babbler." Preaching Jesus and the resurrection he is "a setter forth of strange gods."[12] Yet, after he has spoken Paul manages to create division among the philosophers, some of whom mock him, others prepared to hear more later, and yet still others (a man, Dionysius, and a woman, Damaris) "clave unto him and believed."

Initially, Christianity was never a philosophy among philosophies. Only much later, with Erasmus was it so construed; now among the educated secularists it is not even a philosophy, it is just an ideology, which means any inspirational spark can be dissolved into the structures of the surrounding social complexes. But originally Christianity was something which could take in and dominate philosophy because the love that it taught neither began nor stopped with wisdom, and hence neither began nor stopped with philosophers, nor for that matter with any of the other Greek "wise-guys," the sophists, poets, and orators. Just as the love it taught offered something to the least gifted and least intelligent, the love it taught also extended beyond the people who had come to believe that they alone had been chosen by God—the Jews. The establishment of the centrality of love means simultaneously the fusion of all the Jewish laws into the law of love and the extension of the love beyond the confines of any particular people. To take but one formulation: "Love the Lord thy God with all thy heart, and with all thy soul, and all thy mind…and Thou shalt love thy neighbor as thyself. On these two commandments hang all the laws and the prophets" (Mathew 22:37–40). Faith trumps birth, love trumps everything, and hence a new hope both deeper and broader than anything experienced in the Roman Empire before is opened up. This condensation of everything else into love (all life's depth and all its breadth is in this one power) makes the truth that was, is, and will be accessible to all by virtue of its ground and sheer simplicity. Yet it brings with it a tremendous difficulty in fulfillment; it requires eternal vigilance and the ceaseless testing and surrendering of the self. To surrender the self (a command which is required pretty much by every world religion) means to be open to the divine creative power of love which is, as John says, what God Himself is (1 John 4:8–15). Our capacity to love comes from God who is love; our neighbor is God's image; so we cannot love God without loving our neighbor; in loving our neighbor God's love is revealed to us because this is how we know God; conversely not loving means not knowing God (1 John 4: 7–8). The difference between the Christian truth and the Greek philosophical truth could not be more striking: the act, not contemplation, discloses to us the truth of the highest, though it is in submission to the highest that the act is able to be undertaken. Our love of God feeds our love for each other; our love for each other feeds our love of God; God's love feeds all; but

God's love is also demonstrated by His act which was to send "His only begotten Son into the world, that we might live through Him" (1 John 9). The living presence of the Son means that the highest is tangible in the world. It is exactly the same insight that features (albeit perversely) in all political, sectarian, and, most recently, managerial cults of the personality, the insight that the spirit which is being invoked in order to transform the world requires some visible sign of its presence as a means of activating the energies of its servants. What, however, distinguishes Christ for his believers from the other cult or state leaders is that His divinity is of the one true God who is the God of love and whose command is one of perfecting His love through us; those who serve the god of the nation, the party, or the company always serve a lesser power and by so doing can only ever fail to activate lesser powers in their followers. The supreme power of God is not only that He makes the world, but that He deploys us in the perfection of His power. He sends his greatest gift ("for God so loved the world" [1 John 3:16]) His Son as a sign and living example of this perfection; the word made flesh. To follow Christ, then, is to participate in the perfection of the power of love. This cannot be done unless we love one another; conversely in doing that we love God. Those who do not love a brother or a sister, says John (1 John 4:20), "whom they have seen, cannot love God whom they have not seen"; and by following Christ we see how it is perfectly done, in both his love for the Father and the Father's love for him. In this way one dwells in God and God dwells in one. This, according to John, is the condition that casteth out fear. (Conversely, not being in this condition fills us with fear.) Universal brotherhood was not a doctrine invented by Christians; some Cynics had advocated it and variants of it are discernible in pre-Christian Stoics. What was peculiar to Christianity was its activation of energies which kept the injunction alive, even during times when it was only rarely fulfilled, and in the second millennium flowing out into secular tributaries such as the French and Russian revolutions. What is surprising is not that the uncompromising injunction was and is so often flouted and replaced by the less loving and easier traits of self-righteousness and ethical legalisms, but that it was adhered to by so many who embraced poverty, risked their lives with the sick, and died for their faith.

The importance of the figure of Christ in all of this was, among other things, as a mediative bridge between souls. There was never the command that one should love only fellow Christians, or even one's friends but this love had to extend to the enemy and the persecutor

(Matthew 5:43–44). The body of solidarity between men and women cutting across class, national, gender, racial, and all other lines is the creation of a common faith. Without the faith the act, originally at least, is impossible. Again the what of the faith is all important, and the what is revealed through the living example of Jesus. When Paul says in Corinthians (2. 5:14) that the love of Christ "constrains us," he is indicating the "shape" of love's power: Being Christ-like is being subordinate to God's love, is fulfilling the creative power that can perfect us and make gods of us. That modern men and women wish to be as gods is evident from the elevated role given to the self who is ostensibly sovereign, creator of his or her own destiny. But that the self as such is plagued by its failures is all too evident from the world it inhabits, which does not stop self-help gurus endlessly promising how the self can realize its divinity—i.e., its true nature. In such cases the self-help guru becomes the Christ-like figure for the lost, and the only question is whether it works. But from the start there is one problem—Christ comes to redeem the world, not just the self. A God-like self in a hell-like world might have made sense once and once only—that is how Christianity sees it—but the task is only completed with a second coming.

The meaning of Christian love, then, emanates from these core narrative elements in which God's potency has been revealed: His Son and His creation. Where we do not love right we do not love divinely, we do not emulate the Son, and we do not build the solidarity of loving souls.

Christian ascetic renunciation finds its grounding in the directive of right love: the asceticism of Christ, his apostles and the evangelists stems from the compulsion of creating a body of love. The love is as hard and uncompromising as it is possible to be. It is nothing but giving. Its "logic" is: lovingly giving—the one nonphantasmic form of sacrifice—is the inescapable component of life and love; God has given His Son as a gift/sacrifice (the sacrifice is not because God wants His son murdered, but He knows human hearts—Christ shows this is not what God wants); Christians will never sacrifice an other (like Jesus they must themselves be prepared to be the sacrifice). That sacrifice requires renouncing those desires which can destroy the body of love. In place of bodily pleasure, the first Christians speak of a joy that comes from their experience of God's love and love of their neighbor. The negative weight placed upon the sexual is utterly bound up with the insight into the nature of "suffering creation" as so in need of redemption that only perfect love can make that possible, and perfect love contains sacrifice at its very center.

Contrast this for a moment with the Freudian and post-Freudian view that has largely replaced the Christian one. From the Freudian variant of naturalism the trick is to get the right mix of satisfaction and control (too much satisfaction, no civilization and no achievement; too much control and we are filled with neuroses). At all times, nature, our nature, dictates and must be complied with. The Christian, on the other hand, works from a deep distrust of what nature has become; or rather, what we have made of our nature. The love that we are to respond to is not natural, but divine; the faith that we are to have is likewise not natural; nor is the hope. Here too Christ's actions and presence are signs of the power that creates and perfects nature rather than derives from it. One of the ways this is constantly demonstrated throughout the New Testament is in the miracles. Jesus is a healer and his disciples are instructed to heal through their faith; God can and does overcome nature because his love conquers suffering nature. As Louis Bouyer observes:

> But the miracles of healing, and especially the healings carried out on the Sabbath day, [show] …what God cares about in creation is man, and especially suffering man. It is for his sake that he once again takes creation in hand, so to say. And here he reveals himself with a tenderness, an understanding, a mercy, as near at hand as it is powerful. For man, for fallen man, beaten to the ground, God shows himself so loving that he breaks what seems to be his most sacred ordinances. The God whom the Sabbath honors, himself violates the Sabbath, and he does so for the sake of sinful man. No bounds, then, can be assigned to his love, to his *hesed* [the Old Testament term for God's compassion and mercy] not even the limits that he himself most solemnly established.[13]

Just as the miracle is the correlate of the divine origin of Christ and the divinity of the power that has created Him and that He expresses for the father, the correlates of suffering are sickness, injustice, sin, and demonic possession. Jesus casts out demons because sinful men and women are prone to possession and the subsequent sickness that follows from possession. The demon is the personification of a suffering born of divine defiance and energies that have putrefied. The demon is what sin does; likewise the continuation of the putrefaction is the continuity of the demon, the furtherance of the sin and the depletion of the powers which are required for the perfecting of God's love.

The devil is essentially the absence of right love, as is sin, as is injustice: all are embedded in the closing off from the power that creates life. Perhaps most alien to us is that sickness itself is seen as a sin, and as a punishment. Christ teaches that out of the heart come the good things of the world. On the other hand, death and decay are intrinsic to the world: how to overcome them? That can only be done with spirit which takes what is dead and gives it new life; resurrection of the body is the overcoming of a seemingly undefiable limit; but the act of defiance, unlike the demonic, is in accordance with love. That means that all powers traceable to God are surrendered back to God. In this respect there is a deep affinity between Stoicism and Christianity. But it is equally deep with all paths which are dedicated to overcoming the world of suffering and being with God. Just as we are born without our own assistance we have no choice over the necessity of death in life, but the hope of resurrection is that the loving is eternal as is the lover. Essential to this are the characteristics of Christian love which Paul articulates in the First Letter to the Corinthians (13:4–7): together they are the essential components of surrender: patience; kindness; the absence of envy, boastfulness, arrogance, and rudeness; compliance; the absence of irritability and resentment; rejoicing in truth and not wrongdoing. Love "bears all things, believes all things, hopes all things, endures all things." And the Christian must do this in a world which mocks and kills those who so act: for in the eyes of the powers of the world, surrender is weakness. Nietzsche was right when he saw that the morality of Christianity was grounded in the will to power of the weak, and he was right that the Christians wished to do away with a world dominated by nature's cruelty and the sweet pleasures that could be extracted from it. But, for the Christian, Nietzsche's talk of the strong is just so much hot air. Nietzsche for his part deploys culture as the measure to assess the potency of men, dividing the world, as he does, between the strong and weak. Ultimately, though, neither culture nor the individual is so strong that it too does not find itself conquered by further powers. Nietzsche's paganism consists in his unreal elevation of partial powers. For in a decision no less absurd than the Christians, he resurrects the Stoic doctrine of eternal recurrence as a means of affirming the transitory forever. He says he does so to affirm strength and fill the weak with self-disgust: but his madness is his *hybris*, as if strength and weaknesses were essences that attached to certain natural types. We are all weak; that Jesus himself rebukes the person who calls him "good master" saying there is none good, but one, that is, God (Mark 10:18) is indicative of the Christian emphasis upon where we stand in the scheme of things. Jesus always and only teaches the deference of all powers to the power of God, to the Father; what is done in Jesus's own name is but the way of gathering as a body of love for and in the name of the Father. (That this move easily degenerates into idolatry is not in dispute—but such idolatry does not begin from the lips of Jesus.) To gather beneath or surrender to a lesser power than the Father Himself is to ignore the way of creation; to then make some permanently weaker than others is merely to deplete the collective powers of the species even more. We simply do not know what power can flow through what vessel. We are all vessels and we are all caught up in multiple pathways that flow to and through us. How to facilitate the irruptive flow of powers is the task that creation sets us.

The Christian focus and orientation is, then, on the communion of powers that is achieved through making love the supreme power and alerting us to the obstacles that impede love and hence the communion. At the basis of the great difficulty of the Christian life is that the love that is accentuated overturns all the usual earthly joys: wealth, a full stomach, a good reputation, and even laughter as the false consolations of the world. (Not surprisingly the pagan revival intrinsic to modernity, as is made explicit in Rabelais and Nietzsche, is in large part out of a desperate need to laugh again, after what began as joyful news of salvation had become a grim hospice of sanctimony.) And poverty, tears, and hunger are signs of those deemed worthy by God (Luke 6:20–21). But the poverty, hunger, and tears do not of themselves make worthy, and were that so, everything Nietzsche says of Christianity being grounded in resentment would be incontestable. Rather the conditions of suffering and of not having are but preparatory for the greatest trial of all: loving without any hope of gaining, not judging, always forgiving. The act of deferral, though, is the very condition of receiving: all this giving will have its reward. There has been no shortage of "Christians" who think the rewards promised here are material; heaven as a big department store, no less crude, but equally as stupidly superstitiously carnal as the reward of seventy-two virgins for martyrs of Islam. But while this may have generated "Christians" such a view is neither Christ's nor Christ-like. The reward is purely and simply love itself in a world without end. The love of God, the love for God, and the love of neighbor break open the world ("whoever wishes to be a friend of the world becomes an enemy of God" [James 4:4]) as it has been, requiring a complete recreation of what we value, what we are and what we will be.

Thus far I have attempted an overview of the nature and importance of love in Christianity, but I have skated swiftly over the way in which Christian love is a response to evil, and that what makes this response so powerful is the depth of its understanding of the nature of evil and the drastic means it offers for the way out of evil. Moreover, the depth of its insight flows not simply from the understanding of the first Christians to the world around them, but to their understanding of evil as such, to how evil is active in any time for any group. This is the real testament to its universality, not simply its willingness and desire to include all members into the one body of faith, but in its understanding of what makes a human being (and any human world and human age) fall, and what makes a human being or age flourish. The theory and works of René Girard, and his student, Robert Hamerton-Kelly, as well as Eugen Rosenstock-Huessy's most beautiful book, *The Fruit of Lips*, throw powerful light on how Christianity turns its back on the most "natural" of practices, the practice of finding a victim to blame for the tribulations and violent crises of a community. Moreover, the first Christians were revolutionary Jews in revolt against what they saw as the decline that had taken place in their own faith as well as the various worlds of their environs. This failure was most patently manifest in the fact that it was Jewish authorities and a Jewish crowd that demanded the death of Jesus, and the earliest persecutors of Christians were Jews. That so much persecution by Christians toward Jews has been based upon this is undeniable—and that such persecution contravenes what was specifically Christian (as opposed to the merely "natural" response of revenge) seems to me to be equally undeniable—but the "sins" of "Christians" do not undo the "sins" of the Jews. Put most bluntly we can say that it is of the nature of murder that the murdered haunts the living, and no phantasmic cloak of self-righteousness can stop the ghosts of the murdered haunting the children and grand children of the murderers. For just as today "Christians" are haunted by their complicity in the murder of Jews, the murder of Jesus and the earliest martyrs was to be the great haunting of the Jews of the early Christian era. I do not say this to make a moral point—for the fact of haunting seems to me more primordial than any moral theory or point of view.

61

I take it as indisputable (a) that Christ and the earliest Christians were Jews who were disgusted with what they saw as complicity in the world's evils by powerful people and groups within their own faith, and (b) that Jewish leaders observing Jesus and his followers were understandably fearful of this new heresy and wished to stamp it out. Of the motive and the role of the Jewish high priests and their justification of the murder it is worth quoting John (11:47–53) and Girard's subsequent comment on this passage in *The Scapegoat*:

> Then gathered the chief priests and the Pharisees a council, and said, 'What do we? for this man doeth many miracles. If we let him thus alone, all men will believe on him: and the Romans shall come and take away both our place and nation.' And one of them, named Caiaphas, being the high priest that same year, said unto them, 'Ye know nothing at all, Nor consider that it is expedient for us, that one man should die for the people, and that the whole nation perish not.' And this spake he not of himself: but being high priest that year, he prophesied that Jesus should die for that nation; And not for that nation only, but that also he should gather together in one the children of God that were scattered abroad. Then from that day forth they took counsel together for to put him to death.[14]

Of the passage Girard says, "Caiaphas is the perfect sacrifice who puts victims to death to save those who live. By reminding us of this John emphasizes that every real cultural *decision* has a sacrificial character (*decidere*, remember is to cut the victim's throat) that refers back to an unrevealed effect of the scapegoat, the sacred type of representation of persecution."[15] What Girard underscores is that Caiaphas represents a type—not specifically a Jewish type, but a recognizable human type to be found across the ages and the nations. That his victim will serve a purpose for his people is a most natural way of thinking. Caiaphas is not special, although his role enables him to decide who the sacrifice should be. But the act of sacrificing someone else for a political end is all too typical.

That the crucifixion (and hence the action of Caiaphas) is justifiable from a strictly Jewish point of view was sharply expressed by Franz Rosenzweig in his correspondence with Rosenstock-Huessy when he said: "we have crucified Christ and, believe me, would do it again every time, we alone in the whole world (and 'fiat nomen Dei Unius, pereat homo,' ['let the name of One God exist, and let man pass away'] for 'to whom will you liken me, that I am like?'"[16] Rosenzweig's defense of the crucifixion is a defense of the meaning and sacredness of the Jewish life, but it is precisely the meaning of sacredness that inevitably—in spite of all common ground between Jews and Christians—separates Jews and Christians. What Rosenzweig sees is that the Christian world ultimately would try to destroy the Jewish nation. It is the stubbornness of the Jews who refuse to be swallowed up by the universalistic aspiration of the Christian faith that frustrates the Christian purpose of the forging of a spiritual unity of the human race. Rosenzweig's own refusal to feel apologetic about the Jewish role in the crucifixion is so striking because it expresses precisely what he intends to express—that some things are sacred enough they must be protected unto the death. Equally as interesting as Rosenzweig's provocation is Rosenstock-Huessy's response that "Christ today has people enough in his church to crucify him! It is not true that the Jew today would crucify him—'they alone in the whole world.' For the Jews crucify, judge, condemn no longer!"[17] That is, for Rosenstock-Huessy, part of the success and the truth brought into the world by Christianity, that the genuinely sacred has no need of such a sacrifice, that the spirit works different than man, and this, for him, is evident in the fact that the Jews "crucify, judge, condemn no longer." Another way of saying this is that Jews and Christians have, in spite of their inimical history, learnt from each other.

Of course, Rosenzweig's provocation only draws attention to one party of the crucifixion and Caiaphas is but one who starts the proceedings, but it is not only the priests and Pharisees that are complicit in the murder, but the Roman equestrian procurator Pontius Pilate and the crowd who will not accept Pilate's strategy to spare Jesus. For Girard, the account of Pilate illustrates the power of the crowd—"Once mobilized, the crowd has absolute power, dragging institutions with it until they are forced to disintegrate."[18] It is the combination of the contagion that accompanies mimetic violence and the culmination of that violence that necessitates the search for a way out of the contagion itself that mainly concerns Girard. And his simple observation is that the sacrificial way out is no way out, but simply a myth, an illusion which ultimately enables the continual reproduction of the same energies which endlessly repeat the process of mayhem and murder. For Girard, this very real and seemingly endlessly repeated process is also visible in the process of demonization, and demonic possession, "the result of aggravated mimesis."[19] But what, he notes, sets Jesus apart is that just like his contemporaries he saw and walked among the "possessed." But rather than shun them, or turn violently against them, he "drove out the demons" and left behind the formerly possessed living man. There is no scapegoat. As Girard says of the miracle at Gerasa, which involves Jesus casting out demons who enter into pigs and throw themselves off a cliff (Mark 5: 1–17), "it is not the scapegoat who goes over a cliff, neither is it a single victim nor a small number of victims, but a whole crowd of demons, two thousand swine possessed by demons. Normal relations are reversed. The crowd should remain on top of the cliff and the victim fall over; instead, in this case, the crowd plunge and the victim is saved."[20]

Ultimately it is neither a Jewish nor Roman crowd that is responsible for the crucifixion—it is the crowd as such. Or to put it another way, Christianity holds up a mirror to humankind by showing what it does in its violent mimetic outbreaks. Robert Hamerton-Kelly put the position well when he wrote:

> Theologically speaking, in crucifying Christ the Jews and the Romans acted representatively for all the human race. The essence of anti-Semitism with respect to the crucifixion is to pretend that only the Jews are responsible and not all of us gentiles too, that is, to scape-goat the Jews. The mirror image of this, that it is only the gentiles who are responsible, is equally an act of scapegoating. According to mimetic theory it is an example of the way mimesis makes the rivals into doubles, The Jews who claim innocence are the mimetic doubles of the Christian anti-Semites. Jews and Romans together are responsible, as representatives of all the human race in its violence against the divine.[21]

The act of "indicting" scapegoating as such is tantamount to recognizing that all of us are prone to this "sin"—and for Girard it is "the original sin."[22] Girard's defense of Christianity results from what he sees as unique about the Christian attitude to sacred violence, to scapegoating and the genuine siding with the victims. It requires refusing to be a perpetrator in the condemnation of the innocent—for we are all guilty. Loving the neighbor means abandoning faith in a mythical God who wants us to suffer. We must cease all scapegoating and victim substitution and take responsibility for our own desires and failures. We must hold the mirror up to ourselves and build on the basis of the reality of our shortcomings rather than the mythic delusion of our innocence. Jesus taught that instead of copying each other in our appetitive conflagrations, whilst hiding behind the infinite excuses we allow ourselves but not the other, we must open our hearts to each other. "There is," says Girard, "no other cause for his [Jesus's] death than the love of the neighbor lived to the very end, with an infinitely intelligent grasp of the constraints it imposes."[23]

While Girard was not in any way influenced by Rosenstock-Huessy, the latter's reading of the gospels in *The Fruit of Lips* provides an extraordinary rich account of the central role of violence and victimhood within them. Like Girard, Rosenstock-Huessy emphasizes that the violence is overcome through a revolutionary understanding of victimhood and its relationship to divinity. That revolutionary understanding is also at the heart of the elevated role ascribed by Jesus to love's nature and power. For Jesus, love occurred through faithful speech and action, but says Rosenstock-Huessy, it was the murder of Stephen which, he notes in chapter 4 of The *Fruit of Lips* entitled "Ink and Blood," forced Matthew to take up his pen and write the life of Jesus.[24]

What strikes Rosenstock-Huessy about Matthew's importance—and this is also why he thinks Matthew is the first author of a gospel—is his emphasis upon the sacrificial role of the victim and the new role taken by Christ as victim—a role which simultaneously shows the victimizers to be the very sinners they want the sinner to be, and the victim who shows others what being a victim really means—as opposed to the myths and fantasies which dedivinize and dehumanize through the mystifying process of sacralization of the victim so that he may be the divinely sanctioned victim, and so that the rest may continue to lead the kinds of lives which make the cycle of mimetic violence and victimhood inevitable. As a victim, Jesus is in a familiar role but as a victim who addresses the process from the perspective of the love that is at the source of creation, Jesus's completely destabilizes the process that it would seem he is affirming by willingly becoming the lamb: "Since the Son forewent power for faith, forewent the opportunity of making others suffer instead of suffering himself, he exhibited his proper credentials."[25]

And "Jesus has instituted this process by which means men sacrifice themselves for their enemies, for a society which reacts violently against them. And he who opened men's eyes to this destiny of any child or man, of being 'injected into the bloodstream of society,' is the anointed, the Christ whom all others can follow."[26] And again:

> But by being the voluntary victim, he becomes the first victim in the world who can speak. Nobody had ever spoken in this role. But victims, though mute, were essential. The association between the ancestors and the living was based on the common meal at which the dead partook as though alive, and the whole burial and funeral

rite was based on this association between the dead and the living. The spirits of the dead asked for food, and these ghosts were blood-thirsty if they were not fed, according to the faith or superstition of all tribes... Sacrifices were the core of ritual since they alone incorporated the group and gave it a legal status as a public corporation, beyond the grave, beyond the accidents of birth and death. Sacrifice, then, was the only means of establishing order and of creating legal persons.[27]

That the victim would speak is, suggests Rosenstock-Huessy an act of massive impropriety—a violation of the social rules or etiquette which keep things as they are. Jesus's entrance into the world is revolutionary because it is *revolting*—a violation of good taste, as Rosenstock-Huessy puts it. For the initial revolt was by Jews against the Jews, by Jews of ill taste and ill repute against Jews of good taste and good reputation. This, says Rosenstock-Huessy, was clearly grasped by Matthew who addressed it head on.

> The price of all ritual is sacrifice. When we bind ourselves to a ghost of the past, to a piece of paper, to a house, to a grave, we are apt to spill somebody else's blood for the purpose. And so it is to this day...Jesus created a brotherhood where before the victims had been drafted. But the Eucharist is still a scandal to a Jew. It makes him vomit, quite literally, as it would any man of etiquette. Matthew knew that the pudenda of life were real. That it was less bad taste to speak as the victim, as bread and wine, than to do the act of condemning the Just. He (Matthew) was immune against the mortal disease of good society. He knew that everything has its price. And that nothing is more expensive than freedom from the taboos of good society. And so he ceased to call the first man who had spoken for the victims and as a victim, by his name in society, son of David, Son of Abraham, as he had begun in Chapter One. This taboo was broken, Matthew, in his last chapter found himself in the infinitely more exciting society of sinners who no longer were bound together by high entrance fees but by the name of the first victim who had spoken out loud.[28]

Finally, the law of love and its Christian interpretation involves the reconfiguration of the meaning of blood ritual and the flesh of the offering. The imbibing of flesh of the God spiritualizes the imbibers so that in this most primitive of rites we are reminded of the ingestion of God Himself as the most important of all ingestions, as the true source of the energy that enables us to do His work. Here we can see that the true flow is of love, of God's love to humanity—the Son provides the flow by proving the flesh, lovingly—not now in His death but in His resurrection; death being but the condition of resurrection, the ending of one form of life for a higher form. Here the trust is divine because it is absolute, to use a term which is usually more apt for philosophy, but which is intended here in its concreteness and uncompromising nature. The violence that we are ever entangled in and which ever threatens to break out has found a new outlet in something that is the reversal of itself, but via a rite which symbolizes the most elemental of human qualities—flesh and blood. Though, no blood is spilled and no flesh is torn—it is an ingestion without loss which is miraculous—at least potentially so, if the participants are capable of truly following through in their faith, and imitating the Son.

The Enlightenment view of Christianity was that it was superstition, a substitution racket in which the truth of creation and morality (the only truths that should be divinized)[29] were covered over by rite and ritual and that once a moral had been extracted from it all would be well. But the religion of reason failed to endure for anywhere near as long as Christianity had done so—the deficiency of 'mere' reason was all too conspicuous to many of the brightest of the very next generation who rejected it in favor of a panoply of 'truths' that constituted what became known as romanticism—because it did not grasp that we are creatures of imitation and ingestion, and that morality is but part of a greater process of life-formation.[30] The energies of life must be dealt with, and the energies of violence do not simply dissipate when confronted with reasonableness. Why should they? Life's energies are not particularly rational. What is needed are living bonds and the transfer of energies more powerful than violence. Thus, the church was supposed to be the living, moving body of loving souls, and that love's actuality and expansion required that corporeality and bondage. This did not mean that the church was ever assured of not succumbing to the phantasmic. But, at least in its origin, its power came from the fact that Jesus and his followers had grasped the phantasmic nature of the relationship between violence and the sacred—a new way had been found.

To conclude this chapter let us quote from *The Fruit of Lips* one last time, and another reflection by Rosenstock-Huessy upon Matthew:

> The Mass and the Eucharist, the inner core of all divine services is written up in Matthew.
>
> Since he made it clear that Christ bought, by his sacrifice, the salvation of the sacrificers, it was now written that the victim of every

meal, that [namely] bread and wine, spoke to the dining communion and invited them to shift with their master to the other side of the counter, so to speak, to the side of the victim. In the Mass, every member is invited to be sacrificed or to be ready to be sacrificed for the salvation and the renovation of the world. In the Mass, the first victim invites the others, the partakers, to a service in which they themselves are the offerings. In the dullness of the average mind, this fact rarely makes a dent. People have degraded the divine service to a church parade or a social gathering. But the church was built on the faith that from now on, no divine service was permitted unless the people considered themselves as the sacrifice offered. The whole expression of a Body of Christ, with the head in Heaven, meant exactly this, that we who would crucify the Lord every day, in our rage and envy and indifference, now, with our eyes opened once for what we have done and are doing, declare solemnly: We now, together with our Head, step on the side of the silent victims and offer ourselves to our Maker so that he can remake the sacrifice as he pleases.[31]

"As he pleases"? We know what pleases—love. And it is the depth of his understanding of love that makes Augustine the greatest of church fathers.

Notes

1. Eugen Rosenstock-Huessy, *Out of Revolution: The Autobiography of Western Man* (Norwich, VT: Argo, 1969 [1938]), 508.
2. Anders Nygren, *Agape and Eros*, trans. Philip Watson (New York: Harper and Row, 1969), 62. In his *Star of Redemption*, Franz Rosenzweig goes much further as he makes the case that the key to the teaching of revelation is the formulation from Song of Songs that "love is as strong as death," while the key to redemption is the formulation of love of the neighbor.
3. Forthcoming with University of Toronto Press.
4. Cf. Robert Hamerton-Kelly, "Desire is Imitative and Acquisitive," in *Sacred Violence: Paul's Hermeneutic of the Cross* (Philadelphia, PA: Fortress Press, 1991), 22.
5. Irving Singer, *The Nature of Love: Volume 1 Plato to Luther* (Chicago, IL: University of Chicago Press, 1984), 270.
6. *Theology Today* 29 (1973).
7. Singer, *Nature of Love*, 287.
8. The issue of whether Christians can be homosexuals can be considered in two contradictory ways which go to the heart of biblical interpretation and Christian practice. The first involves a consideration of specific passages where homosexuality is addressed, and it is clear that it is one further transgression to be condemned, much like adultery of incest. The second involves the elevation of the central command of the New Testament to love God and one's neighbor over the specific proscriptions. Those proscriptions are then considered in the light of historical and cultural context. They retain

their absolute validity only to the extent that they are not inconsistent with the commands to love. Along these lines, the argument can be made that the conditions under which the proscriptions against homosexuality were articulated no more hold than most of the other proscriptions outlined in such detail and whose transgressions are punished with such severity in Leviticus and Deuteronomy. Many of those commands are either simply seen as irrelevant today such as the details on hair and beard grooming (Leviticus 19:27–28), or even contrary to the spirit of the New Testament—consider the proscription against the deformed offering food to God (Leviticus 21:16–23). Hence the transformation of sexual mores which has led to a greater practice and acceptance of homosexuality means that to simply equate homosexuality with sin is simplistic. The strength of this argument is its dynamic interpretation of spirit, something accentuated time and time again in the New Testament, though the mobility of God's law is equally evident in the Old Testament. This argument does not change the historical fact that homoeroticism, as Plato's Greece illustrated, was a cultural choice which the Jews and then Christians specifically condemned and hence rejected as inconsistent with the way they wished to operate. The traditionalist response to this is that this is in violation of the fact that we are made in God's image, and God has fashioned woman as man's partner. Ultimately, the argument revolves around how literally and how freely in spirit one interprets the Bible. Both conservative and liberal readers of the Bible accentuate one of two features whose combination and original inseparability gave the Bible much of its power: the imperative voice of God which gives direction, a voice which is not to be questioned and subjected to rational interrogation (the conservatives), and the impossibility of those commands being strictly adhered to because all but the overarching commands of love refer to specificities which are constantly taking on a new meaning (the liberals). The liberals rightly see that there is simply no such thing as a hundred percent literal interpretation of the Bible (an insight central to even non or preliberals such as Augustine); on the other hand, the conservatives rightly fear that our desire all too easily smothers God's words as we substitute the comfortable satisfaction of our desires for the stringent requirements of salvation. Having said that, I find it difficult to see how those who judge and persecute people who really love because of the way they love are acting lovingly rather than fearfully. On the other hand, the positive aspect of erotic desire seems to play no part at all in the books of the New Testament.

9. See also *Paul to Romans* 1:18–32.
10. G. Rattray Taylor, *Sex in History* (London: Thames and Hudson, 1953), 257.
11. Ibid., 265.
12. It should also be mentioned that "poetry" is not mentioned in the Bible, and the reference to "poets" appears only once in the New Testament, also in Acts. That is to say, the Jewish and Christian mindset is not easily dissolved into the more Greek one of poetry and philosophy.
13. Louis Bouyer, *The Spirituality of the New Testament, Volume 1 of A History of Christian Spirituality*, trans. Mary Ryan (Minneapolis, MN: Winston Press, 1960), 48.

14. I cite the King James version, John 11:47–53, Girard does not use the King James version.
15. René Girard, *The Scapegoat*, trans. Yvonne Frecerro (Baltimore, MD: John Hopkins University Press, 1986), 114.
16. Eugen Rosenstock-Huessy, *Judaism Despite Christianity: The Letters on Christianity and Judaism between Rosenstock-Huessy and Franz Rosenzweig*, with an introduction by Harold Stahmer and essays "About the Correspondence" by Alexander Altmann and Dorothy Emmet, (Tuscaloosa, AL: University of Alabama Press, 1969), 113.
17. Ibid., 141.
18. *Scapegoat*, 106.
19. Ibid., 172.
20. Ibid., 179.
21. Hamerton-Kelly, *Sacred Violence*, 11.
22. Cf. Ibid., 197; Cf. Girard, *I See Satan Fall Like Lightning* (Maryknoll, NY: Orbis, 2001), 150–51.
23. Girard, *Things Hidden Since the Foundation of the World*, trans. Stephen Bann and Michael Metteer (Stanford, CA: Stanford University Press, 1987), 211.
24. Ibid., 29.
25. Ibid., 57.
26. Ibid., 55.
27. Ibid., 67.
28. Ibid., 68–69.
29. Thus, the predominance of deism in the Enlightenment, which reduces religion to symbols of the creation of nature and morality.
30. One docs not need to be an Hegelian to appreciate that the importance of ingestion was not lost on him.
31. Ibid., 70, 72.

3

The Loves of St. Augustine and the Church: Religion plus Philosophy plus Politics*

The history of Christianity is a history of contesting interpretations, power politics, and all the accompanying victories, defeats, intrigues, compromises, and loss of purity that characterizes the hell of the political realm combined with flashes of Christ-like lives and inspirations. At almost every step in its political development a cost was paid for by its spirit. Nevertheless, there was a strange providence at work—on the one hand, the more Christians there were and the more Christian the earthly kingdoms became, the more Christ's teachings were compromised with the worldly; on the other hand, the message of love of neighbor spread through all the capillaries of the body of Christendom, even as Christians raped and pillaged and enslaved in the name of Christ. Christ had provided the measure for neighborly love, for he had originally brought into union the act of sacrifice and the articulation of the command. In each and every age where Christianity had been, the world and the age were deficient when this measure was applied. That it would be so is not remarkable given the example and requirements of discipleship laid down by Jesus (giving up wealth, embracing the poor and a life of poverty, being with and healing the sick, overcoming any transgressive sexual desire and, for those who would be witnesses to the good news, renouncing all sexual desire and family life to marry oneself to Christ, forgiving everybody, not judging, acknowledging that we are all sinners, serving all.) What is miraculous is that a movement dedicated to such a lifeway was so successful for so long. It is true, though, that had it not been for Augustine, its success may have been restricted to the first four hundred years after Christ's death, which would, to be sure, have been no slight thing.

71

Augustine is the most important political figure in the construction of the West. It was he who most profoundly directed the church into the Middle Ages, he who did not merely dream of a thousand-year Reich as Nietzsche did in his *Also Sprach Zarathustra* (not to mention Hitler whose thousand-year Reich lasted but twelve years), but who provided the definitive theoretical basis, steering a middle course between the uncompromising religious strictness of the Donatists and the ascetic-philosophicalism of the Pelagians, for an institution whose reign lasted a thousand years and beyond. Augustine achieved this while living on the perimeter of the new spiritual imperium as Rome was being sacked. He closely observed the great empire in its gasping condition, while passionately entering into the doctrinal skirmishes and collisions which threatened to tear the church apart. He was the most extraordinary amalgam of capacities in a world and a time pulling in such potentially different directions. As a soul burning in belief, he burns almost as bright as St. Paul; as an intellect he displays a mind almost as philosophically luminous as Plato, from whom he learnt so much; as a man involved in the great social direction of his day with an uncanny ability to grasp the historical significance and potential of competing doctrinally motivated groups, one has to wait until Lenin until one reaches someone as sensitive to what the moment requires politically as Augustine; though unlike Lenin, Augustine's ideas had staying power. In one overwhelmingly important respect it can be plausibly argued that Augustine was not Christ-like. Augustine invokes the state to use its powers to punish heretics in order to save the unity of the church, like Luther (forever linked with his anti-Semitic rants and blood-curdling call to slaughter the rebellious peasants) and Calvin (forever associated with the cold-blooded deceits leading to the murder of Michael Servetus) and other men living in violent times aspiring to create social peace, the violence of the times stuck to his thinking. One does not have to believe in Christ to see that Christ's "genius" was his ability to flow as if untouched by the world's desires. While with Christ and the martyrs, the violence of the times was ingested by love in the faith and hope that love itself would rebound into the future and change the times, by the age of Augustine, the weight of love had become heavier because of the gravitas that is the inevitable accompaniment of anyone who carries organizational, institutional/political responsibility.

However one judges Augustine as a Christian, it remains the case that his life's work was devoted to strengthening the only institution that he believed could bring humanity into one family and create a universal fellowship and a universal history. Augustine, as Peter Brown rightly says, conceived of the human race "as a vast organism, like a single man, that changed according to a pattern of growth that was inaccessible to the human mind, yet clear to God."[1] But that organism had, under paganism, remained a sick being periodically tearing into itself. The church, for those like Augustine, was the divine gift that alone could achieve a unity of peace that no emperor or king had done. It was the Corpus Christi, the living presence of the resurrected Christ on earth. The church was the incarnation of souls joined in heaven-directed love under the sign of the suffering God, whose suffering was the very result, not of God's creation, but of human evil. Augustine's great hope, then, was that the body created out of divine love realized through the faith of Christ's disciples "might become coextensive with human society as a whole: that it might absorb, transform, and perfect, the existing bonds of human relations."[2] We get a powerful sense of Augustine's hope from his following address to the church:

> It is You who make wives subject to their husbands…by chaste and faithful obedience; you set husbands over their wives; you join sons to their parents by a freely granted slavery, and set parents above their sons in pious domination. You link brothers to each other by bonds of religion firmer and tighter than those of blood. You teach slaves to be loyal to their masters…masters…to be more inclined to persuade than to punish. You link citizen to citizen, nation to nation indeed. You bind all men together in the remembrance of their first parents, not just by social bonds, but by some feeling of their common kinship. You teach kings to rule for the benefit of their people; and it is You who warn the peoples to be subservient to their kings.[3]

It has often been noted that when Descartes subjected everything to radical doubt and then concluded that he could not doubt that he was doubting and hence that he was a thinking being that his search for an indubitable foundation to take humanity into a future free from the quagmire of the past was, in fact, a repetition of an argument of Augustine's. It is an interesting fact that the founding father of the medieval church and the founding philosopher of modernity would make the certitude of their thinking so important in their respective metaphysical strategies. But as Augustine's argument demonstrates, what separates the two is that this thought, when deployed by Descartes, bears no relationship to love, whereas in Augustine it is inconceivable without it. His argument to the Academicians, who ask, "What if you are deceived?" is as follows:

> For if I am deceived I am. For he who is not, cannot be deceived; and if I am deceived, by this same token I am. And since I am if I am deceived, how am I deceived in believing that I am? For it is certain that I am if I am deceived. Since, therefore, I, the person deceived, should be, even if I were deceived. Certainly I am not deceived in this knowledge that I am. And, consequently, neither am I deceived in knowing that I know. For, as I know that I am, so I know this also, that I know. And when I love these two things, I add to them a certain third thing, namely, my love, which is of equal moment. For neither am I deceived in this, that I love, since in those things that I love I am not deceived; though even if these were false, it would still be true that I loved these false things. For how could I justly be blamed and prohibited from loving false things, if it were false that I loved them? But, since they are true and real, who doubts that when they are loved, the love of them is itself true and real?[4]

As is evident from this passage, for Augustine we are always in the midst of love, and what we love and what loves us is what makes us. Ultimately, it is not overstating the case to say that the originality of Augustine's thought, and indeed the thought behind all his thought, is expressed in his oft-repeated formulation: "For the specific gravity of bodies is, as it were, their love, whether they are carried downwards by their weight, or upwards by their levity. For the body is borne by its gravity, as the spirit by love whithersoever it is borne."[5] We are never a pure subject or pure object but a never-ending reconfiguration whose patterning is dependent upon what comes toward us. That love makes and destroys us stands in the closest relationship to Augustine's idea of how God's love and grace may transform our sinful acts through providence. It is because God is a God of love that grace and providence may always trump sinful human history, which does not mean that we always respond to these greatest of divine gifts. We may choose to struggle on loving our destructive loves. Indeed, life is a struggle of loves; though our loves, when not touched by grace, are blind, self-serving and damaging. This is also why Augustine constantly reminds men and women of their paltriness in the faces of the forces that makes them. In a passage that adumbrates the mechanists' doctrine of self-preservation and Nietzsche's will to power, Augustine speaks of the eros within nature that creates the violent struggle between its parts as each blindly seeks its own continuance:

> [D]o not even all irrational animals, to whom such calculations are unknown, from the huge dragons down to the least worms, all testify that they wish to exist, and therefore shun death by every movement in their power? Nay, the very plants and shrubs, which have no such life as enables them to shun destruction by movements we can see, do not they all seek in their own fashion to conserve their existence, by rooting themselves more and more deeply in the earth, that so they may draw nourishment and throw out healthy branches toward the sky? In fine, even the lifeless bodies, which want not only sensation but seminal life, yet either seek the upper air or sink deep, or are balanced in an intermediate position, so that they may protect their existence in that situation where they can exist in most accordance with their nature.[6]

This drive for existence may embroil humans in a deathly struggle or else it may open outward and upward to provide the sustenance and endurance, the immortality, that is blindly striven for. What we become is ultimately decided by what we willingly serve, by what we love. That we all must serve something/somebody is, for Augustine, a fundamental condition of life. Love is service. The corollary of this is that we never really serve what we do not love; the slave, for example, may be forced to serve a loathsome master, but such service is not done with the heart, and thus not a service of the self or soul, but merely of the misfortune of earthly circumstance. What we love is the great question that confronts each and every one of us, the key to our world and self-making. That is also for Augustine why the will takes on such existential importance. For the free will is "the right will" and that is well-directed love; concomitantly, the wrong will is ill-directed love. The task of the will is to give or hold assent from the four fundamental forces that reconfigure and activate us, that is, that attract our love. These forces are "first, that which is above us; second, ourselves; third, that which is on a level with us; fourth, that which is beneath us—no precepts need be given about the second and fourth of these."[7] To love in this order is to love rightly.

The first of these objects of love is God who is "that which excels in dignity all other objects."[8] He is the perfect being, the perfect object of our love. His "eternity is true," His "truth is eternal," and His "love is eternal and true" and "He Himself is the eternal, true, adorable Trinity, without confusion, without separation."[9] "There alone is our love not in danger of going amiss, not misplaced, able to provide complete fulfillment. There our being will have no death, our knowledge no error, our love no mishap."[10] When, then, we love God we are drawn to Him and our soul is no longer weighed down by the impulses and pulls of the material body in its attractions for material things. Being infinite God is that which cannot be loved too much. Indeed, love of God is the purpose of our existence, just as we are created from out of God's love. And the good life is quite simply one spent in the love of God—"What," he asks, "is the chief end of man?" to which he answers: "To glorify God and enjoy Him forever" (for from that love all else will follow, including the love of neighbor). As he writes in *On Christian Doctrine*:

> For this is the law of love that has been laid down by Divine authority: 'Thou shall love thy neighbor as thyself;' but, 'Thou shall love God with all thy heart, and with all thy soul, and with all thy mind,' so that you are to concentrate all your thoughts, your whole life and your whole intelligence upon Him from whom you derive all that you bring. For when He says, 'With all thy heart, and with all thy soul, and with all thy mind,' He means that no part of our life is to be unoccupied, and to afford room, as it were, for the wish to enjoy some other object, but that whatever else may suggest itself to us as an object worthy of love is to be borne into the same channel in which the whole current of our affections flows.[11]

In her early work *Love and Saint Augustine*, Hannah Arendt neatly summed up the essence of Augustine's contrast between this right love and the false love when she said: "Augustine calls this right love *caritas*: the root of all evils is *cupiditas*, the root of all good is *caritas*" (*Commentaries on Psalms* 90:1, 8). Hence, Augustine warns, "Love, but be careful what you love" (*Commentaries on Psalms* 31:5).[12] *Caritas* is inseparable from purity of heart. And, in spite of Augustine's willingness to concede the necessity of force to stamp out heresy, fear of punishment is not a component of *caritas*.

> Thus the end of every commandment is charity, that is, every commandment has love for its aim. But whatever is done either through fear of punishment or from some other carnal motive, and has not for its principle that love which the Spirit of God sheds abroad in the heart, is not done as it ought to be done, however it may appear to men.[13]

This false love, *cupiditas*, breeds a self that is disconnected from the dignity and order of life. It is a love that folds in upon itself, craving its own at the expense of the other, a self-love that is the opposite of the love that a self needs to be a healthy self, a selfish love that is but the projection of a falseness of self. As Nygren says, for Augustine "'self-love' is not merely one sin among others, but the sin of sins."[14] It is the sin of sins because it is an enclosure that violates the creative spirit of life, pulling us in and down into decay, and thereby depriving us of the capacity of loving spiritual flight, which for Augustine is the very purpose of life and divine love. Thus, we are ever moving between our loves and when we do evil it is because our *cupiditas* has obstructed *caritas*. As Augustine says: "What is it that effects even the evil in man, if not love? Show me a love that is idle and effects nothing. Vices, adulteries, crimes, murders, all kinds of excesses—is it not love which produces them?"[15]

"Love, then, yearning to have what is loved, is desire; and having and enjoying it, is joy; fleeing what is opposed to it, it is fear; and feeling what is opposed to it, when it has befallen it, it is sadness. Now these motivations are evil if the love is evil; good if the love is good."[16] For Augustine, then, the motivations themselves are neither good nor evil. Being above fear is not a good in itself, for not fearing God may be a sign of hubris. Likewise, feeling sorrow, something, he points out, that the Stoics think is something only for those who are not wise.[17] But this very example is indicative of the folly of those who would call themselves wise and yet not know what the emotions are for. Not understanding the value of emotions the Stoics avoid them, and in their avoidance they lack compassion and hence the possibility of real fellowship.[18] In this respect the philosophers are not good men,

> so long as we wear the infirmities of this life, we are rather worse men than better if we have none of these emotions at all. For to be quite free from pain while we are in this place of misery is only purchased, as one of the world's literati perceived and remarked, at the price of blunted sensibilities both of mind and body.[19]

Moreover, they are said to be in the grip of "stupid pride" because they fancy:

> that the supreme good can be found in this life, and that they can become happy by their own resources, that their wise man, or at least the man whom they fancifully depict as such, is always happy, even though he becomes blind, deaf, dumb, mutilated, racked with pains, or suffer any conceivable calamity such as may compel him

77

to make away with himself; and they are not ashamed to call the life that is beset with these evils happy.[20]

Evil, according to Augustine, is not in the nature of the world as his Manichean former brothers and then enemies taught—for God created nature, and nature is the visible proof of God's majesty,[21] rather we choose evil, which is "but the absence of good,"[22] because we love the wonderful things of God's creation, the world, more than we should, and thus ignore what is of far greater worth. As he says in *The City of God*: "the defection of the will is evil, because it is contrary to the order of nature, and an abandonment of that which has supreme being for that which has less."[23] Indeed, were the world not good, there would be no evil.[24] Men and women, then, in their striving after and serving the lesser become slaves to what is a small part of a greater plan, and mistaking a part for the whole, they become captive to what is there for them to take joy in, insofar as they realize the real nature and source of God's creation. "He who inordinately loves the good which any nature possesses, even though he obtains it, himself becomes evil in the good, and wretched because deprived of a greater good."[25] But that is precisely what is lost in choosing the lesser over the greater, the temporal over the eternal, driven by lusting after what is hurtful and ignorant about our own condition. In this diminished condition of self-feeding off self and trying to steal what is a gift calamity piles upon calamity:

> This is the first evil that befell the intelligent creation, that is, its first privation of good. Following upon this crept in, and now even in opposition to man's will, ignorance of duty, and lust after what is hurtful: and these brought in their train error and suffering, which, when they are felt to be imminent, produce that shrinking of the mind which is called fear. Further, when the mind attains the objects of its desire, however hurtful or empty they may be, error prevents it from perceiving their true nature, or its perceptions are overborne by a diseased appetite, and so it is puffed up with a foolish joy. From these fountains of evil, which spring out of defect rather than superfluity, flows every form of misery that besets a rational nature.[26]

Longing to keep and fearing to lose what either God would that we should not acquire or retain,[27] for Augustine, they do all manner of unworthy things to keep what is by its nature unkeepable. For all things of the world are by their nature perishable. The human heart, though, is righteous and is doing God's will when it is faithful to/works/serves/

creates/acts (these are all synonyms when done in the right spirit) in a manner which is in keeping with love of God. That is to say, Augustine appreciates that love of God is bound up in the double fellowship of humans with God and humans with humans in Christ, with their *imitatio* of what is but love's incarnation. The righteous deeds which the gospels require all boil down to the fact that one does not twist one's behavior in order to get what one wants, one does not sacrifice one's soul for an outcome such as money or sexual satisfaction or glory or whatever it is that one desires. To place oneself beneath any one of these "goods" is to tear oneself apart from the commandments of love. This, then, is the great paradox of excessive self-love: it is self-destructive. The real issue for Augustine was what one loved most: the self as self, or God. And the love of self which overreaches itself, becomes so that it really does "hate itself."

> For, however far a man may fall away from the truth, he still continues to love himself, and to love his own body. The soul which flies away from the unchangeable Light, the Ruler of all things, does so that it may rule over itself and over its own body; and so it cannot but love both itself and its own body.
>
> Moreover, it thinks it has attained something very great if it is able to lord it over its companions, that is, other men. For it is inherent in the sinful soul to desire above all things, and to claim as due to itself, that which is properly due to God only. Now such love of itself is more correctly called hate. For it is not just that it should desire what is beneath it to be obedient to it while itself will not obey its own superior; and most justly has it been said, "He who loveth iniquity hateth his own soul." And accordingly the soul becomes weak, and endures much suffering about the mortal body. For, of course, it must love the body, and be grieved at its corruption; and the immortality and incorruptibility of the body spring out of the health of the soul. Now the health of the soul is to cling steadfastly to the better part, that is, to the unchangeable God. But when it aspires to lord it even over those who are by nature its equals—that is, its fellow-men—this is a reach of arrogance utterly intolerable.[28]

In his attack upon self-love, it is not that Augustine is preaching the ascetic's doctrine of self-laceration. That too is but another trick of the self to draw attention to itself, to make it the center of the universe's attention. For Augustine, love of the self must be according to its real due; it must not receive a dangerously exaggerated sense of importance, as also with love of the world. By its nature the self can never really hate itself (for even that self that commits suicide because it is unhappy with its lot, seeks to be free of the burdens so that it can be at peace with itself). Hence he argues that "there is no need of a command that each man should love himself."[29]

> Now he is a man of just and holy life who forms an unprejudiced estimate of things, and keeps his affections also under strict control, so that he neither loves what he ought not to love, nor fails to love what he ought to love, nor loves that more which ought to be loved less, nor loves that equally which ought to be loved either less or more, nor loves that less or more which ought to be loved equally. No sinner is to be loved as a sinner; and every man is to be loved as a man for God's sake; but God is to be loved for His own sake. And if God is to be loved more than any man, each man ought to love God more than himself. Likewise we ought to love another man better than our own body, because all things are to be loved in reference to God, and another man can have fellowship with us in the enjoyment of God, whereas our body cannot; for the body only lives through the soul, and it is by the soul that we enjoy God.[30]

We have already alluded to the fact that for Augustine the church provides a vehicle of fellowship unlike any other known to the human race. Insofar as it is dedicated to the love of God, it is absorbed by what transcends the world and hence is not subject to the world. In this all-important respect, for Augustine, the Christian faith offers a hope beyond all other hopes for what fellowship can achieve.

In terms of this all-important principle, or, better, body of fellowship, the only body that is remotely comparable to the church is the state. But, for Augustine, the demise of Rome shows what becomes of states—and reading Augustine on the demise of states, one cannot help but be reminded of Scipio, at his moment of victory over Carthage as he watches the city he has conquered burn, weeping for Rome's future. That, for Augustine, is the fate of earthly powers.

That the logic of ancient empires was ever bound up with a belief in their own eternity, and favor by (the) God(s) was something all too evident to Augustine. The prophet Daniel had prophesized that a new empire would come which would end the cycle of empires, which is to say he had foreseen that death must not always conquer the life of peoples, but such a reversal of nature was based upon God and an openness to God's love. This idea was taken up by Augustine in his understanding of the church and it would, as Rosenstock-Huessy argues in his *Soziologie*, involve the church in a radical reinterpretation of the relationship between God and imperial power. No more would this or that territorial empire be able to be seen as the domain of God's favor and representation, but rather the church had made time and not space the real vehicle of the Holy Spirit's presence within empires. Thus, the transition and translation of God's spirit in the world would be appreciated as ever moving between empires, but as ever continuous within an empire that was not an empire, the holy church. This doctrine would be known as *translatio et imperii*. This stands in the closest relationship to the Christian emphasis upon time and incarnation of new creative acts of love taking priority over space and the ruling of powers which are ultimately and literally dead ends.

But there is more to the demise than the circularity of life energies which is so fundamental to the pagan view of life world that even Plato must concede that his ideal state if realized on earth must enter into decline. There is a fundamental difference at the center of each institution: one is grounded in self-love; the other "love of God in contempt of one's self to the heavenly city. The first seeks the glory of men and the latter desires God only as the testimony of conscience, the greatest glory." The name Augustine gives to these two cities, the earthly city and the city of God, point, of course, to the respective goals and goods between which humans can choose. That Augustine's depiction of the *Civitas Dei* is a means for assessing the defects of the terrestrial city is often considered part of his Platonic legacy. And that legacy is very much in evidence when we see that Augustine's *Civitas Dei* is not simply the visible church, a point nicely made in John Figgis's lectures, *The Political Aspect of Augustine's "City of God,"* when he says it

> is the *communio sanctorum*, the body of the elect, many of whom are to be found in pre-Christian times or in heathen peoples, while from this body many among the baptized will be excluded. This *communio sanctorum* is the true recipient of the promises to David and of the gifts of eternal peace and beatitude, those promises which Augustine sets forth with moving eloquence in Book XX [of the *Civitas Dei*]. The visible Militant Church is never more than a part of either—nor does it ever attain. Its peace and beatitude are in hope. It is always in via. It is but the symbolic and inadequate representative of the *Civitas Dei*, but it uses the peace provided by the earthly State.[31]

That is, the *Civitas Dei* is not simply the visible church—when in obedience to God, it is heavenly, when it itself is enmeshed in the same forces as the earthly city, it becomes part of the earthly city.

For Augustine, the distinction between the two cities can be seen in the one's love of ruling as opposed to the other's love of serving (love of divine love). The earthly city is bound up with forced servitude, torture, injustice, and war. Earthly cities are founded by fratricide and robbery (and "what," he asks, "are robberies themselves, but little kingdoms?"). Being bound to the earth it cannot achieve its ends without the contradictions that are part and parcel of a life that is based upon its inversions of the proper order of life: to achieve peace, it must violently conquer that which opposes peace. The stark dichotomy Augustine makes between these two cities is at once a condemnation of the love of the world which has become detached from the love of the source which feeds it, thereby creating realms of injustice, selfishness, and violence. The citizen who gives all loyalty to the earthly city will find himself condemned to creating a future that will never be more than cycles of violence and stolen joys. The citizen of the heavenly city will always live as a stranger in the earthly city: in the world, but not captive to worldly things.

It is often said and true that there is something of Plato in Augustine's division, but it is also the expression of his dissatisfaction with those philosophical aspirations that reach from Plato to Cicero and Plotinus for a just order under the God of reason. For Augustine, justice can only rule where the divine order is in place:

> The function of justice is to assign each his due; and hence there is established in man himself a certain just order of nature, by which the soul is subordinate to God, the body to the soul. And thus both body and soul are subordinate to God.[32]

A pagan principality (even if it were to be ruled by just philosophers) always must be captive to the idolatry of its ground; the worship of a power, even a noble one (say Justice itself taken as the end, or Reason as God) rather than love and the God of love who expresses His love through self-sacrifice and redemption.

Augustine is, then, not conciliatory to other gods and philosophies to the extent that they would pull men and women once more into the energies and limited range of institutions which made the pagan world so tormented.[33] He is conciliatory to the extent that those truths which they contain be integrated into the strategy of the church and the universal fellowship of faith, hope, and love. In this respect, Augustine even says: "a man who is resting upon faith, hope, and love, and who keeps a firm hold upon these, does not need the Scriptures except for the purpose of instructing others." And elsewhere he will simply say "Love God and do what thou will."[34]

In conclusion, Peter Brown sums up beautifully the Augustinian social vision when he writes:

> The members of the *civitas peregrina* [the city of resident strangers] therefore, maintain their identity not by withdrawal, but by something far more difficult: by maintaining a firm and balanced perspective on the whole range of loves of which men are capable in their present state: "It is because of this, that the Bride of Christ, the City of God, sings in the *Song of Songs*: '*ordinate in me caritatem*.' 'Order in me my love.'"[35]

Notes

*   Some of the material in this chapter has appeared in a different context in my "The Weight of Love and Evil in Augustine," in *St. Augustine: His Legacy and Relevance*, ed. Wayne Cristaudo and Heung-wah Wong (Adelaide: Australian Theological Forum, 2010).

1.   Peter Brown, *Augustine of Hippo: A Biography*, (Berkeley, CA: University of California Press, 1967)317.

2.   Ibid., 224.

3.   *De mor.eccl.cath.* (I), xxx, 63 in Ibid., 225.

4.   St. Augustine, *The City of God* trans. Marcus Dods, in *St. Augustine's City of God and Christian Doctrine*, (Edinburgh: T&T Clark, 1871), 11:26.

5.   *City of God* XI:17, also *City* 11:28 and St. Augustine, *The Confessions*, trans. R.S. Pine-Coffin, (Harmondsworth: Penguin, 1961), (13:9) where he writes: "love is the weight by which I act. To whatever place I go, I am drawn by love. By your Gift, the Holy Ghost, we are set aflame and borne aloft, and the fire within us carries us upward."

6.   *City* 11:27.

7.   On *Christian Doctrine* trans. J. F. Shaw in *St. Augustine's City of God and Christian Doctrine*, (Edinburgh: T&T Clark, 1871) 1:23.

8.   Ibid. 1:7.

9.   *City of God* XI:17.

10. Ibid.

11. On *Christian Doctrine* 1:21.

12. Hannah Arendt, *Love and Saint Augustine*, edited by Joanna Scott and Judith Stark, (Chicago, IL: University of Chicago Press, 1998), 17.

13. St. Augustine, *Enchiridion* trans. J. F. Shaw, in *On the Holy Trinity; Doctrinal Treatises; Moral Treatises*, (Edinburgh: T&T Clark, 1956), 121.

14. Anders Nygren, *Agape and Eros*, trans. Phillip Watson, (Chicago, IL: University of Chicago Press, 1982), 537.

15. Ennarr. in Ps.XXXI.ii. 5 in Ibid., 494.

16. *City* 14:7.

17. *City* 14:8.

18. Cf. *City* 9:4 and 5.

19. *City* 14:9.

20. *City* 19a:4.
21. *Confessions*, bk. VII, 12.
22. *Enchiridion*, chap. 11.
23. *City* XII:8; Peter Brown makes the good point that Plotinus provided a way out of the Manichean conception of evil, which the young Augustine adhered to, in *Ennead* 1, viii, 15 (MacKenna 2, 78) where he says "Evil is not alone: by virtue of the nature of good, the power of Good, it is not Evil only: it appears necessarily bound around with chains of Beauty, like some captive bound in fetters of gold: and beneath these it is hidden, so that while it must exist, it may not be seen by the gods, and that men need not always have evil before their eyes, but that when it comes before them they may still not be destitute of images of the Good and Beautiful for their Remembrance." Brown, *Augustine of Hippo*, 99.
24. *Enchiridion*, chap. 13 and 14.
25. *City of God* XII:8.
26. *Enchiridion*, chap. 24.
27. *Enchiridion*, 81.
28. On *Christian Doctrine* 1:22–23.
29. Ibid. 1:39, chap. 35.
30. Ibid. 1:chap. 27, para. 28.
31. J. N. Figgis, *The Political Aspects of Augustine's City of God* (London: Longmans, 1921), 68. now online at http://www.sacred-texts.com/chr/pasa/chap04.htm (accessed January 5, 2012).
32. *City of God* XIX, 4.
33. On *Christian Doctrine* 1:39:43.
34. *Homily 7 on the First Epistle of John*, para. 8.
35. Brown, *Augustine of Hippo*, 325.

4

The Medieval Return
of Venus

On Sunday April 25, AD 1227, crowds gathered at every crossing
along a road on the Italian mainland near Venice, to watch an extraordinary procession pass by. It had been thoroughly advertised
in advance by a messenger bearing an open letter to all the knights
of Lombardy, Austria, and Bohemia. The letter stated that on April
24, the goddess Venus would arise from the sea near Venice and start
the next day to travel north to Bohemia, breaking lances with every
warrior who would meet her in the lists.[1]

Thus, Morton Hunt, in his *The Natural History of Love*, describes
Venus's return to Europe. It was not without significance that Venus
was, in fact, a man, a knight-poet, Ulrich von Lichtenstein, author of
the *Frauendienst*, or *Service of Women*. His appearance typified the
return of a type that Christianity, with considerable success, had largely
sought to eliminate, viz., the lover. St. Augustine's *On Marriage and
Concupiscence* had taken a more tolerant approach to sex than that
advocated by other sects such as the Manicheans, Montanists, Mar-
cionites, Basilidians, Saturninians, Valesians as well as other church
fathers like St. Jerome.[2] But, nonetheless, he took a grim view of the
pleasures of the body—the sexual organs were unruly and failed to
conform to the will; sexual union was given by God solely for the
purpose of procreation; sex, within marriage for pleasure alone was
a venial sin (outside of marriage it was a mortal sin); concupiscence
could not be avoided in the sexual act; and, perhaps most tortured
of all, was his "reasoning" that original sin is transmitted through
the lusts of the parents. The latter claim would return to plague how
Augustine would be seen by Protestant and post-Christian Western
generations, who thought that the church's struggles against the flesh
tended only to dehumanize it by making it an instrument of control
and obsession. It is a pity that those who know little of Augustine

85

tend only to see him through this lens. But he himself contributed to this picture. Granted that this was the case, though, one must also concede that in the midst of the monumental breaking down of the known world, sexual gratification was not a force that offered much for rebuilding. It should not be surprising that in a world that seemed to collapse due to its carnality and cruelty that the church's rebuilding was heavily based upon ascetic emphasis upon renunciation, and a predominantly patriarchal vision. Though, as Peter Dronke in his *Medieval Latin and the Rise of the European Love-Lyric* has noted, the feminine energy had been venerated in the Sapiential Books of the Old Testament (the Books of Wisdom, Proverbs, Solomon) and that, in the early years of Christianity, a number of Gnostic sects were "full of…fantasies of love-unions and cosmic syzygies," and the belief in "a mystic marriage," while in the Hermetic text, Asclepius, the creator must be both male and female.[3] But with few exceptions, the triumphant orthodoxy in the West suffered from the inflexible rule of the Father. Venus, and her son, Cupid, had been consigned to the demonic.

We can only wonder how many lives were ruined through patriarchal inflexibility, but I think the correspondence of Heloise and Abélard depicts the savagery and cruelty of a world in which fear of passionate love could entomb a soul as beautiful and alive as Heloise. For those unfamiliar with the story, Abélard was a kind of superstar philosopher and theologian, a dazzling lecturer who attracted students from all over Europe, as well as the author of many metaphysical, logical, and theological and ethical treatises, not to mention significant innovations in music. Perhaps, his most influential work was his *Sic et Non* (*Yes and No*) which had formed the basis of the scholastic method by laying down the fundamental contradictions of the teachings of the church which required the kind of dialectical conclusions that St. Thomas's *Summa* excelled in. His innovations in metaphysics were groundbreaking for their time. He attacked the predominant Platonic belief that universals were real, arguing, somewhat like Aristotle, that all reality was grounded in particulars and that universals were essentially a semantic byproduct of reasoning; he also played a seminal part in introducing Aristotle into universities, and thereby refashioning what was then the fledgling university paradigm, and providing the foundations of what would subsequently become the dominant paradigm of the Middle Ages.

The radical and controversial nature of the metaphysical innovations can be easily overlooked in light of the subsequent success of his method and the centrality of Aristotelianism, generally to scholasticism. But the very method which was to become so prominent in theology, and which was greeted with enthusiasm by students flocking to this "new" way of thinking, was also often viewed with great alarm and suspicion by many of his contemporaries who saw his teachings as heretical. Thus, was he accused of the Sabellian or modal monarchianism heresy—i.e., the belief that the trinity consists of three different modes of one God rather than three distinct persons in the one God. And he found himself being hunted by the notorious inquisitor, but complex and pious Bernard of Clairvaux, himself the author of an important Medieval work *On The Love of God*, who smelled the seeds of the faith's destruction in the new rationalism propounded by Abélard.

It was at the height of his fame—and prior to some of his greatest theological conflicts—that he was to seduce the beautiful brilliant young Heloise, first by convincing her uncle and guardian, Canon Fulbert, that she should study with him, and then moving into Fulbert's household. She quickly fell in love with him and began a torrid and secret love affair. In an attempt to legitimate the relationship, and Heloise having born a son, Abélard sought Fulbert's assent (which he received) to wed Heloise. She was most reluctant to do so believing both that his philosophical pursuits would be burdened by matrimony and, rightly, that this would only damage his career and give ammunition to his enemies. And there were many enemies—indeed he seemed to have a habit of collecting them, beginning with his first teacher William of Champeaux. As he recounts in his *Historia Calamitatum* (*The Story of My Misfortunes*), his teacher turned on him because he had refuted "certain of his opinions, not infrequently attacking him in disputation, and now and then in these debates I was adjudged victor."[4] Then he went to study with Anselm of Laon, only to find the situation more or less repeating itself.

If his teachers took offense at his brilliance, in Heloise he found someone who unconditionally loved him and his talents. And she was not going to let her own needs for security hold him back. Thus, among her arguments against marriage, what Abélard calls her final argument, is the one that more than any other has elevated her in the history of love as a tragic figure of extraordinary passion and devotion. As Abélard tells the story, she insisted

> that it would be dangerous for me to take her back to Paris, and that it would be far sweeter for her to be called my mistress than to be

known as my wife; nay, too, that this would be more honourable for me as well. In such case, she said, love alone would hold me to her, and the strength of the marriage chain would not constrain us. Even if we should by chance be parted from time to time, the joy of our meetings would be all the sweeter by reason of its rarity.[5]

In a later letter, and in what is perhaps her most famous and notorious statement to posterity, she will express her passionate convictions about the downside of marriage with even more vehemence—"if Augustus, emperor of the whole world, saw fit to honor me with marriage and conferred all the earth on me to possess forever, it would be dearer and more honorable to me to be called not his empress, but your whore."

This preference for the honesty, or what we moderns might call authenticity, of passionate love over the domestic confines of marriage is one that would echo through the ages and eventually be the very argument that would legitimate cohabitation outside of marriage. It would be a position she would repeat throughout her extraordinary letters to him. Moreover, and uncannily, Heloise prophesied that their marriage would seal their doom. It did.

The marriage was held in secret, with Fulbert and a few friends there. What happened next is what would make the story of Abélard and Heloise a tale of love for all time.

> We departed forthwith stealthily and by separate ways, nor thereafter did we see each other save rarely and in private, thus striving our utmost to conceal what we had done. But her uncle and those of his household, seeking solace for their disgrace, began to divulge the story of our marriage, and thereby to violate the pledge they had given me on this point. Heloise, on the contrary, denounced her own kin and swore that they were speaking the most absolute lies. Her uncle, aroused to fury thereby, visited her repeatedly with punishments. No sooner had I learned this than I sent her to a convent of nuns at Argenteuil, not far from Paris, where she herself had been brought up and educated as a young girl. I had them make ready for her all the garments of a nun, suitable for the life of a convent, excepting only the veil, and these I bade her put on.
>
> When her uncle and his kinsmen heard of this, they were convinced that now I had completely played them false and had rid myself forever of Heloise by forcing her to become a nun. Violently incensed, they laid a plot against me, and one night while I all unsuspecting was asleep in a secret room in my lodgings, they broke in with the help of one of my servants whom they had bribed. There they had

vengeance on me with a most cruel and most shameful punishment, such as astounded the whole world; for they cut off those parts of my body with which I had done that which was the cause of their sorrow. This done, straightway they fled, but two of them were captured and suffered the loss of their eyes and their genital organs. One of these two was the aforesaid servant, who even while he was still in my service, had been led by his avarice to betray me.[6]

The decision by both Abélard and Heloise to marry in secret was, in part, an essential component of the tragedy, just as the secrecy of the marriage of Romeo and Juliet is also the essentially tragic ingredient of their love. It is worth pausing upon this for the fact that secrecy can be so dangerous tells us much about ourselves. In the case of Abélard and Heloise it is clear that Fulbert is outraged because he perceived that Abélard has shunned his niece, and, in spite of the anger Heloise directs at him and her kin, he is, nevertheless, outraged for her. He simply cannot understand that there is a kind of loving sacrifice that is not the "normal" kind of sacrifice—it is the sacrifice of the gift. Such a sacrifice may well be viewed, as it inevitably will be by some feminists, as worthless, as a typical instance of a woman giving up herself to a rather unworthy man. This is not how Heloise saw it—for she lived in an environment, which for all its cruelty, patriarchy, and phantasmic religiosity—was deeply steeped in the idea of loving service. And she saw Abélard's loving service toward philosophy as something essential for doing the Lord's work, just as her loving service was toward him. On this front, it cannot be said she was wrong. For each was engaging in a gifting form of nonphantasmic sacrificial love. That it was enormously painful for her—far more for her than for him—we learn from her letters. But that it was done with a loving heart and devotion is not in question. But Fulbert does not and cannot see this. For he thinks like someone *outside* a loving–gifting relationship—and that loving and gifting takes place as if behind a veil; one cannot see it unless one has enough heart to open one's eyes to something most unusual. Thus, his thinking is of the crowd and it turns swiftly to violence—to the violence of honor that (he thinks) Heloise and he himself as a member of her family feel in the shunning and shame he perceived to come from Abélard. It is that sense of violent imitation that drives him to "rectify" the situation in the most elemental form of violent reciprocity.

It is a strange truth about love that the spiritual magnificence of the action of the lover is not necessarily dependent upon the quality of the beloved. Of course, to be lovingly idolatrous toward a murderer may simply be loveless indifference to the sufferings of others. Loving devotees of the mass murdering political monsters are still stupid and callous in spite of their love because they are willfully blind. The real lover *looks* to what makes the beloved capable of more loving deeds. Nevertheless, the lover is not deficient because he or she does not love a perfect person, even a person who may lie or cheat, possibly even murder. The lover does not fail in love when they see and still love in spite of the beloved's sins, and they may love enough to lift the beloved to become the potential that the lover sees within them. There is a thin line between love and fantasy, but it is still a line.

The sacrifice of one's own "needs" so that the beloved may be more giving to the world is one of the oldest and most powerful dimensions of love. Traditionally a case can be made that it may have been more often done by women (though the ultimate sacrifice of men in battle required to protect their territory and family should make us steer clear of generalizations). But it is only with the modern insistence upon the realization, fulfillment, and comfort of the self that such lives are seen somehow as deficient, as if the modern feminist is the pinnacle of self-fulfillment, while other women were mere dunces, dupes, and slaves—a view which is but one more trope in the logic of Enlightenment. One does not need to deny that it is good for all people to enhance their capabilities in order to be better, or wealthier in spirit—but it is simply a delusion to think that by *having* more power, and opportunities one is ipso facto either enriching oneself or others.

There is one simple question that must be asked if one believes that the spirit of love is more venerable than the spirit of selfishness or empowerment when one is adopting any pursuit—"by doing this am I putting more love into the world?" We might rephrase the question for the modern preoccupation with the Self by asking—"by doing this am I more lovable?"

Ingestion of opportunity, of wealth, of power is nothing more than ingestion. It is no great end, and leads to no great place. Love always seeks a greater place, a greater end. All the "ism" and "ist" ideologies of modernity, be they capitalist, socialist, feminist, conservative, racist, antiracist or whatever are all serving the same dead end if they do not make the world and the practitioners more lovable. And whereas those ideologies which preach domination of the Other are, at least in the postholocaust context easily shown to be catastrophic, other ideologies which emphasize equality and moral virtue are all too often not less conspicuous in their lovelessness. And lovelessness is still lovelessness, and the loveless life devoted to equality and progress eventually shows itself as loveless and tragic as any other loveless life. Ideas and doctrines do not generate love. This digression is I think particularly pertinent in an age where the political and moral high-ground—taken in the name of the victim—is so commonly taken to condemn far more loving and nuanced deeds and lives that occur upon different social–cultural and historical terrains. And is it not also conspicuous how quasimetaphysical appeals to differences of culture and historical context are just another riff in the hyperbolic moralizing of the self-serving victim advocate?[7] Likewise, is it not all too conspicuous now that so many of the radicalized men and women who grew up in the 1960s and felt that they were missing out, and that the world and themselves would be better by having more are often embittered and angry because they are no different than the rich and privileged who they have criticized and have become? When Erich Fromm insisted upon the difference between being and having, in *To Have or To Be* (1976), and the superiority of the former, he was already sensing that the radical ideas of self-transformation that he and others had been developing for so many years, and which were to play an important part in the counter culture were in danger of creating a generation no less lost than their parents. Let us bear this in mind before we simply judge Heloise.

For in the case of Abélard and Heloise, I think it fair to say that Heloise's love for Abélard cannot be judged on the basis of his own relative neglect of her needs; for their love was never reciprocal. Abélard's first love was precisely what he most sacrificed himself for—viz., philosophy, while Heloise's first love was Abélard. And while their names are linked with each other in the history of tragic romance, Abélard's immortalization is first and foremost through his philosophy, while Heloise's through her love for Abélard. Thus, it was that Abélard reports that after his castration, what overwhelmed him most was the

> disgrace more than the hurt to my body, and [I] was more afflicted with shame than with pain. My incessant thought was of the renown in which I had so much delighted, now brought low, nay, utterly blotted out, so swiftly by an evil chance. I saw, too, how justly God had punished me in that very part of my body whereby I had sinned. I perceived that there was indeed justice in my betrayal by him whom I had myself already betrayed; and then I thought how eagerly

my rivals would seize upon this manifestation of justice, how this disgrace would bring bitter and enduring grief to my kindred and my friends, and how the tale of this amazing outrage would spread to the very ends of the earth.[8]

The rest of their story is one of Abélard's continual devotion to God and philosophy, and Heloise's suffering struggle with her enforced vocation, a struggle made all the more difficult by what seems to be Abélard's belief that God had punished their love through the instrument of Fulbert and his henchmen. When contact was established again between the two, what is so striking is how obsessed (if I may use this term in a nonpejorative manner) Heloise is with Abélard, and how distant Abélard is from her. He has left his passion behind and directs all his energy to his religious/philosophical life—she is left with no choice and the remainder of her life will be devoted to the convent, of which she has become the abbes, and her further promptings of Abélard in friendship and instruction. One may well read the letters between the pair after their "re-uniting" as the sublimation of passion—but this would be to take Abélard's more Platonized Christian gloss on the tragedy rather than hear the slow and suffering acceptance that comes from Heloise's voice, a voice more buried in her convent than free to serve love's spirit. What we hear in Heloise is Venus herself wanting to break out of her confinement, and the church (and the castrated Abélard) locking her up yet again. Perhaps, Heloise had shown that Venus could not return yet as a woman, and then she could only make her way back into the world through a man and in a spiritualized form, as she did via Ulrich von Lichtenstein, and as she would in the courtly love tradition.

There are many theories about the origin and even the appropriate name that should be given to that poetic and chivalrous Medieval movement which was built around "honest love" (*amour honestus*) and "refined love" (*fin amour*) and, which, in the nineteenth century, received the name courtly love. De Rougemont argued in his controversial classic *Love in the Western World* that it was a dualist heresy inspired by the Cathar male mystics who, while striving to free themselves from the evils and burdens of their bodies, lived in loving friendship with women, and had learnt the ecstatic joy of the tantrics. Alexander Denomy argued that it was a naturalistic heresy, fittingly in a little book entitled *The Heresy of Courtly Love*, and its philosophical roots can be found in the Arab fusion of neo-Platonic and Aristotelian ideas such as are found in Avicenna's *Treatise on Love*.[9] And the elevation of female beauty to mystical heights suggests a reworking of the Platonic (substituting a woman for the male beloved) and Aristotelian (striving for a good). In the introduction to his translation of Andreas Capellanus's *The Art of Courtly Love*, John Jay Parry states that "for all practical purposes we may say that the origin of courtly love is to be found in the writings of the poet Ovid."[10] Certainly, if the relative sumptuous lifestyle of some of the French courts provided the site for its occurrence, it would seem to confirm Ovid's remark in his *The Remedies for Love*, "So does Venus delight in idleness."[11]

For his part, C. S. Lewis, in *The Allegory of Love*, held that courtly love arose as a "rival" and "parody of the real religion."[12] While Peter Dronke takes the line from a poem, ca. 1200, *Le lai de l'oislet*, "God and Love are in accord" as the key to his reading of the meaning of the courtly love tradition.[13] Basing his argument on lyric poetry from Egypt, Byzantium, Georgia, Mozarabic Spain, and Islamic poetry of the eighth and ninth centuries, he makes a strong case that courtly love was not unique to the troubadours of France and Minnesingers of Germany. He could have added Ts'ao hsueh-ch'in's *Dream of the Red Chamber* from China or Murasaki Shikubu's *The Tale of Genji*, as Otavio Paz does when he makes a similar point about the various geographical locations of the mood.[14]

But what was peculiar to the West was that not only was courtly love taking place "outside the official religion," and often in opposition to it, it made a mass movement of romantic love.[15] Certainly with the troubadours and the Minnesingers, the love lyric had become embedded in European culture—and even though its popularity would ebb and flow, De Rougement is making no overstatement when he writes that:

> The whole of European poetry has come out of courtly love and out of the Arthurian romances derived from this love. That is why our poetry employs a pseudo-mystical vocabulary, from which, quite unaware of what they are doing, persons in love still draw today their most commonplace metaphors.[16]

The Jungian psychologist Robert Johnson states baldly that "[r]omantic love is the single greatest energy system in the Western psyche."[17] And if we considered the sheer amount of time, creativity, labor, and resources that are devoted to the "produce" grounded in romantic love—the relevant areas of teen and women's magazines, popular music, literature, film, television shows, jewelry, greeting cards, florists, honeymoon suites, and package deals and so forth, one would have to concede that Johnson is probably right. Likewise, his accompanying claim that "[i]n our culture it has supplanted religion as the arena in which men and women seek meaning, transcendence, wholeness and ecstasy." No wonder that our age has created never-ending battalions of psychologists and psychiatrists to counsel people through the disappointment of not finding their wholeness in a romantic union. But just as the early Christians tapped into love's power only to have the demonic spirits of fear, rigidity, faithlessness, cruelty, hypocrisy, excessive control, and sanctimoniousness parade under the guise of the commandment of neighborly love, the outbreak of romantic love in the West cannot just be judged on the cultural infantilism that we are so steeped in. The chivalrous steps of romantic love, so often themselves naïve and juvenile, combined the mystic and the eternal and the contingent. But above all, it elevated the feminine after such a protracted banishment, and the movement was so attractive that the church could not ignore it. And could it not respond that it had always a mother of God? Certainly a hymn from the sixth century (which was translated in the ninth century in the West and from the end of the eleventh century was taken up widely) indicates Her importance in the Byzantine church:

> Hail, you state of love surpassing all love…who bring the contraries together…you who contain the divine Sapientia and are a token of God's providence, You who show the philosophers lack wisdom, you by whom the myth makers are made foolish…Principle of the sublime creative power, bestower of the divine bounty. For you have renewed those who were bereft of their minds, you who have given understanding to those who strayed before, your bridal bed of the immortal marriage.[18]

From such a hymn one can see how Dante and other mystic lyricists were tapping into a deep current of faith that had long been given expression within parts of the Christian tradition.

The rejuvenation of the symbolism of the church as a response to the new dominance given to the feminine is one indication of just how powerful and pervasive the energy was. But the church could work with (capture) only a part of that energy. When the troubadour Bernard von Ventadorn sang "By nothing is man made so worthy as by love and the courting of women, for thence arise delight and song and all that pertains to excellence. No man is of value without love,"[19] he had concisely expressed the new faith and the new passion. The troubadours and Minnesingers sang of their beloved as if they were God Himself, and as if the transitory phase of beauty were eternal. Those words of every second pop song which one hears today "I will love you forever" confirm the West's cultural incorporation of the mystical symbolism lying in the heart of the movement. But it would be foolhardy to think that this code of such passionate transgressions were not contradictory, and that a passion and vocabulary in large part derived from and explored with a more detached humor in Ovid did not contain the seeds of Augustine's dreaded concupiscence, as is evident from Andreas Capellanus's late twelfth-century manual *The Art of Courtly Love*.

Andreas was a chaplain privy to the romantic behaviors that had taken on cult status at the courts of Countess Marie of Troyes/ Champagne and her sister Eleanor of Aquitaine. In *The Art* the worldly wise cleric, Andreas advises his friend Walter, drawing upon examples chosen from courtly adjudications on love by Queen Eleanor and Countess Marie, "that it does not do the man who owes obedience to Venus' service any good to give careful thought to anything except how he may always be doing something that will entangle him more firmly in his chains."[20] Andreas courses a very fine line between experienced lover and celibate; on the one hand, drawing attention to all the heady joys (and dangers) of love, and, on the other, of giving lip service to orthodox doctrine. *The Art* reveals a man well aware that, in spite of the church, people, including the clergy, enjoy having sex. In his chapter entitled "The Love of Nuns" after telling Walter emphatically to stay away from nuns because it is a mortal sin, he muses on his lucky escape from a nun whom he had excited with his discourse about love. He concludes: "Be careful, therefore Walter, about seeking lonely places with nuns or looking for opportunities to talk with them, for if one of them should think that the place was suitable for wanton dalliance, she would have no hesitation in granting you what you desire and preparing you for burning solaces, and you could hardly escape the worst of crimes, engaging in the work of Venus."[21] It is hard to believe that Walter would have been chastened rather than spurred on by such prospects of transgression. And, while stating that clerics should not be lovers, Andreas adds that if they must, they should consort with a woman whose station is in accordance with the rank of his parents. Andreas then reveals himself to be worldly wise and the culmination of his wisdom is a list of thirty-one rules such as "He who is not jealous cannot love; That which a lover takes against the will of his beloved has no relish; No one should be deprived of love without the very best of reasons; The easy attainment of love makes it of little value; difficulty of attainment makes it prized; A new love puts to flight an old one." But just as Ovid had spurned love with his *Remedies*, Andreas (whether sincerely as Denomy argues, or not, as Parry and Dronke, in my view, more persuasively, hold) provides a rejection for Walter as he points out that the worldly love of a woman, though natural, is deficient compared to the love of the heavenly God. "No man," he warns, "so long as he devotes himself to the service of love can please God by any other works, even if they are good ones. For God hates, and in both testaments commands the punishment of, those whom he sees engaged in the works of Venus outside the bounds of wedlock or caught in the toils of any sort of passion."[22]

As renunciatively orthodox as such warnings are they must be placed alongside other advice such as when Andreas approvingly cites the judgment that "a marital union does not properly exclude an early love except in cases where the woman gives up love entirely,"[23] and his report of the Countess of Champagne's answer, when asked whether true love can find a place between husband and wife, that it cannot:

> For lovers give each other everything freely, under no compulsion of necessity, but married people are in duty bound to give in to each other's desires and deny themselves to each other in nothing. Besides, how does it increase a husband's honor if after the manner of lovers he enjoys the embraces of his wife, since the worth of character of neither can be increased thereby, and they seem to have nothing more than they already have a right to?[24]

The contradictions in Andreas seems to have been the contradictions of the age—the contradiction between a God of Love who sacrificed His Son and who creates a world where there seems no respite from sacrifice and renunciation, and a goddess who intoxicates, who gives a pleasure that is best accessed through prolonged delay and that, as in the case of Tristan and Iseult, is death itself. If I speak of contradiction it is not in search of a Hegelian resolution, for the contradictions within the medieval experience of love are the fundamental human ones of desire and its fulfillment, of immediate fulfillment and delayed gratification. But they take on such grand proportions because of the renunciative backdrop of its reflexive culture. As the age draws to its end there are tales of sheer sensuality as in Boccaccio and Chaucer and Jean de Meun's naturalistic matter-of-factness in his additions to Guillaume de Lorris's *The Story of the Rose* where he holds that nature wants the male to get to it and help her proliferate. With de Meun, who also draws on ancient tradition, as Julia Kristeva notes, it is nature which is worshipped and courtliness and love which is opposed. As Kristeva says, de Meun signals the arrival of another type: didactic, moralistic, bourgeois—the antithesis of the troubadour and "the first French scientific and philosopher poet who has a 'seventeenth-eighteenth century aura.'"[25] But it is nothing as mundane as procreation which concerns the troubadours and Minnensingers. The troubadours and Minnensingers sing, or as Kristeva, again, nicely phrases it, their "utterance act" is a "speech that is sung."[26] Quite rightly, as in pop songs of our time, and "at their limit" "courtly songs neither describe nor relate. They are essentially messages of themselves, the signs of love's intensity."

Over and over writers emphasize the specialness of the beloved and her meaning, of the dangers of the beloved granting her favor too quickly, of the ecstasy that comes from waiting and undertaking the trials on her behalf. Frequently the lover is restricted merely to a sign or gesture, then a gift, then a deveiling so that the beloved may just be gazed upon in her nakedness, lain with and caressed. And the *fach* (the fact, of copulation),[27] if at all is only after all this courtship. That the relationship is adulterous only serves to highlight the difficulty of accessibility; infrequency (in some cases there is no meeting, at other times, a death bed meeting) and freedom of choice, as opposed to mere marital, and hence routine, duty (Heloise's reasoning is repeated) also underscore that such love is to be prized—is, indeed, a prize. The lines between divine union and union with one's lady are often completely blurred so that Venus's love takes on the meaning of life. Perhaps, not so different from our own time where popular culture and café conversation seem to overwhelmingly converge in the judgment that the meaning of life is a good relationship. Except that then God was not dead and the idea that the gesture of a woman was a divine gesture, and the belief that eternity was to be found in the service to or embrace of a woman was a fantastic reassemblage of the symbols of the age, while the myth of romance in our time shows itself to be tired and stale, and its rightful place is the fantasy of the screen, the pop song and the glossy gossip magazine—for it can barely be found in real life, except as a moment that has no greater longevity than the romantic marriages of the stars.

The church fathers, for all their own lurid fears of sexuality, were not completely wrong to see the demonic aspect of the goddess and her son: for kingdoms, families, individuals, a point made with such power by Dante in the fifth canto of the *Inferno*, have not infrequently tumbled under the energies generated by Venus. And the Greeks already knew that Aphrodite and Eros (the Trojan War, for example) were frequently the bearers of trouble, of evil.[28]

That is to say, Venus was not, nor could be the God of Love. Yet her return was symptomatic of the failure of the love of the one-sided, other-worldly, future-directed, renunciative, sacrificial, patriarchal God of Love to fill the human heart. Only by uniting Her with Him could Love be complete.

Notes

1. Morton Hunt's *The Natural History of Love* (New York: Anchor, 1994 [1959]), 132.
2. For a good case for Augustine's "relative moderateness" on this issue see Alan Soble's "Correcting Some Misconceptions about St. Augustine's Sex Life," *Journal of the History of Sexuality* 11, no. 4 (October 2002): 545–69. Chapter four of Morton Hunt's *The Natural History of Love* provides a lively account of the church's hostility to the flesh. On the positive side, Christianity had protected the widow and the orphan, the abandoned and the fragile. It had inculcated a sense of familial responsibility by its strict line on divorce, and its opposition to prostitution and concubines, again, considered in its historical context, offering advantages to many women whose economic, legal, and social condition was so precarious and dependent upon male protection. It had channeled the passion of strong and intelligent men and transported it away from conquest of the exterior and into conquest of the interior (thereby, of course, conquering the exterior in another manner). It had offered a sense of spiritual purposefulness and relative social safety. It had created a common center for worship. But it had also spread guilt, misogyny, religious intolerance including a legacy of anti-Semitism from Origen's, St. Cyprian's, Gregory of Nyssa's, St. Augustine's, and John Chrysostrom's vitriolic attacks upon the Jews to early church councils' attacks and Christian emperor's imposition of anti-Semitic laws through to outright pogroms.
3. Dronke, *Medieval Latin and the Rise of European Love-lyrics* (Oxford: Clarendon, 1965), 89–90.
4. Peter Abélard, *Historia Calamitatum: The Story of My Misfortunes*, trans. Henry Adams Bellows, http://www.fordham.edu/halsall/basis/abelard-histcal.html (accessed June 4, 2010).
5. Ibid.
6. Ibid.

7. Again I find Girard's frequent observations about political correctness to be apposite. To some critics his position is conservative, but the terms conservative and progressive are but the means to protect a certain kind of privilege and practice, labels to promote another mode of mimetic rivalry and scapegoating.
8. Ibid.
9. Ibn Sina (Avicenna) *A Treatise on Love*, trans. Emil Fackenheim, *Medieval Studies*, Vol. 7, 1945.
10. Andreas Capellanus, *The Art of Courtly Love*, introduction and trans. John Jay Parry (New York: Columbia University Press, 1941), 4.
11. Ovid, "Remedies," in *The Art of Love*, trans. Rolfe Humphries (Bloomington, IN: Indiana University Press, 1960), 186, line 146.
12. C. S. Lewis, *The Allegory of Love* (Oxford: Oxford University Press, 1958), 18.
13. Dronke, *Medieval Latin*, 5.
14. Octavio Paz, *The Double Flame: Essays on Love and Eroticism* (London: Harvill, 1996), 29.
15. Ibid., 30.
16. *Love in the Western World*, trans. Montgomery Belgion (Princeton, NJ: Princeton University Press, 1983), 151.
17. Robert A. Johnson, *The Psychology of Romantic Love* (London: Arkana, 1983), xi.
18. Dronke, *Medieval Latin*, 92.
19. From *Bernard von Ventadorn, seine Lieder*, ed. Carl Appel (Halle, 1915) in Denomy, 59
20. Capellanus, *Art of Courtly Love*, 27.
21. Ibid., 143–44.
22. Ibid., 187.
23. *Art*, 171.
24. Ibid., 107.
25. Julia Kristeva, *Tales of Love*, trans. Leon Roudiez, (New York: Columbia University Press, 1987), 295.
26. Ibid., 281.
27. Paz, *Double Flame*, 80.
28. The notion of Greek sexual carefreeness, part Christian invention and part modern fantasy, is well and truly refuted by Bruce Thornton's Eros: *The Myth of Ancient Greek Sexuality* (Boulder, CO: Westview, 1997).

5

Dante's Divine Comedy: The Heavenly Romance

It is not without good reason that Dante is invariably seen as the culmination of the medieval attempt to reconcile the competing traditions of poetry, philosophy, and religion. He combines the ancient insights into the power of love in their classical and Christian forms with the new myth of romance. The result is a philosophical, religious, political, prophetic love poem where love of a particular woman, love of wisdom, love of justice, love of the language, in general, and poetry, in particular, conspire to demonstrate love of God and God's love. It is not the case that after Dante there is nothing more to be said or sung about love, and Dante knows that the human heart is transported by the melodies of its soul and that love, like an epic or great lyric poem, patterns, modulates, moves, and soars. But there has probably never been such an integrative, beautiful, wise, elaborate, personal yet universal account of love as what Dante provides in *The Divine Comedy*. It is a journey from simple lostness to hell to purgatory to paradise, a journey of descent and ascent, which comprises the worldly and the mystical, personal and social salvation, the private confession that is also a public condemnation of all the evils of the age as well as an inventory of the damnable and potentially perilous behaviors whose roots are to be found in the heart's misdirected loves.

Dante is the penultimate type to emerge from within Christendom. He remains committed to the end that united Jesus, Paul, and Augustine, viz., the creation of a fellowship of love based upon surrender to the God of Love. Yet he also belongs, partly at least, to the romance and troubadour tradition which has introduced the pair of lover and beloved into Christendom as a spiritual entity. The trouble of the coupling of Christianity with lovers is perhaps no more evident than in the pattern of recantation that occurs as the troubadour ages and takes on a cleric's life within the church. Petrarch's final reflections on his beloved Laura are typical: she would have been the spiritual death of him had he not awoken to the dangers of such love; he has lost days and nights spent raving.[1] Boccaccio's late misogyny is a more general example. Although both these examples are post-Dante (and both are, of course lovers of Dante), at the moment they do this they break with the new path that Dante had set. For Dante unites troubadour and church, the beloved and Christ, as much as he unites philosophy and poetry, pagan and Christian mythology (as humanists will subsequently do to an even greater degree). For Dante, love is triumphant and there is no need for such denial, provided the love is followed through beyond the perishable possibilities of this life.

If one line may be said to sum up and underpin the entirety of *The Divine Comedy*, it is the poem's concluding line "the love that moves the sun and the other stars." There is nothing that is not moved by love and this is as true of the creation of the mineral, vegetable, and animal kingdoms as it is for humanity. All is part of a mutual order, a cosmos that is purposeful and god-like.[2] From Thomas Aquinas, Dante had learnt that love's power of animation is threefold: natural (*amor naturalis*), sensory (*amor sensitivus*), and rational (*amor rationalis*). As Kurt Vossler writes: "The stone that falls to earth obeys the *amor naturalis*; the beast that seeks its food or the continuance of its species, the *amor sensitivus*; man who uplifts himself to God, the *amor rationalis*."[3] But Dante's concern in the *Comedy* is not nature as such, but human beings, the creatures who are animated by all three loves and who have the ability to choose rationally what they love and thereby make their future and achieve a good life. The future that had heretofore been made, that is the present in which Dante was immersed was one whose overriding characteristics were discord and corruption. The huge gap between Augustine's *Civitas Dei* and the church visible of Dante's time is almost the first thing that strikes any reader of the *Comedy*. The fact that the first soul witnessed in the vestibule of hell is Pope Celestine V signals in no uncertain manner the importance and extent of the rottenness of much of the church and the place it plays in a world on the verge of collapse. Throughout the *Comedy*, Dante singles out popes and cardinals for damnation, just as, in purgatory, he witnesses excommunicated souls (Manfred of Sicily and Buonconte da Montefeltro)[4] whose valorous actions on earth have made them candidates for salvation. Likewise, he discourses, frequently and repetitively, on the damnable character of simony, on the hypocrisy, avarice, degeneracy of holy orders, and, perhaps most damnably of all the church's complete transmogrification of what Dante sees as its legitimate and valuable role of spiritual Shepherd into a secular political authority. Everywhere the contemporary church of Dante's time is revealed to be immersed in and soiled by its love of the worldly goods of wealth and political power. In the *Comedy*, both the Franciscan and Dominican orders (founded, inter alia, on the vow of poverty little more than a hundred years before the *Comedy*) are castigated for their swift degeneracy and hunger for money. The church has become the beast of Rome: Roma the demonic inversion of *amor*, as the Cathars, reportedly, would put it.

Dante stands at the close of one world and the opening of another. The church survives beyond Dante but the question is: is it necessary beyond Dante? Is the solidarity that it sought to engender absolutely dependent upon its survival? Or is it just a medium for the spirit of the divinity of love? These are not such straightforward questions to answer, and its roles have to be considered against vastly different contexts. Its potency and dignity in Poland and East Germany in the 1980s, or its role in Central and South America and Africa in the twentieth and (early) twenty-first centuries bear next to no relation with what Dante and Rabelais, respectively, confronted in fourteenth-century Italy and sixteenth-century France. Nevertheless, the Protestants of the sixteenth century would see the church visible as nothing but an impediment to and a perversion of Christ, only to find members of subsequent generations interpret not only them and not only Christ, but the very idea of God himself as an impediment to love's divinity. Some authors, such as the great literary theorist Erich Auerbach, and Gertrude Leigh, see Dante as a pioneer of secular thinking. The problem with a complete acceptance of that position is the depth of mysticism, more precisely neo-Platonism, in Dante, which is consistent with an eschatology involving transcendence, and the continuation of the soul in the beyond. That is, in Dante love is conceived as moving worlds within worlds, as an immortalizing power. Yet, it is also the case that Dante is a believer in an eschatology of this world. What for so many people today tends to be a tension between the either/or of the natural and supernatural in Dante is a union of worlds, of here and beyond, both being the creations of that love that moves the sun and other stars.

What makes Dante so difficult, if not completely inaccessible, to so many from our age is the Catholic mental architectonic, is that in spite of the uncompromising attacks upon the corruption within the church, it is as wholeheartedly and powerfully embraced by Dante as the church visible is renounced and attacked by the Reformers who so frequently attack the same corrupt acts as Dante. While, then, Dante is steeped in orthodox Catholic patterns and symbols for understanding the meaning of the life of the soul, the *Comedy* is also guided by the historical vision of the prophet Joachim de Flore (or Fiore) (ca. 1135–1202) (placed in paradise by Dante),[5] who announced that a new age of the spirit was dawning which would be one of universal peace, a Sabbath of the church, under the governance of spiritual intelligences, contemplative monastics dedicated to the service and love of God and humanity. As Gertrude Leigh, in her *The Passing of Beatrice: A Study in the Heterodoxy of Dante*, noted, Joachim's prophetic writings about a little over a century before the *Comedy*, were highly esteemed by a number of popes and his writings on the three ages of the spirit were sanctioned as orthodox by a papal bull early in the thirteenth century.[6] In 1234, another bull dealing with the canonization of St. Dominic, "equated the Florensians with the Benedictines, Cistercians, Franciscans and Dominicans."[7] Joachim taught that there were three ages of the spirit: the first being the age of the Father which was an age of law and fear; the second, the age of Christ and his apostles, which was one of grace and faith; and the third being the age of the Holy Spirit, which was to be an age of love and liberty. While there is dispute among Joachamite scholars about the precise nature of the church's overhaul (it becomes completely secularized thus doing away with the sacraments and clergy altogether as Leigh claims, or, as Bernard McGinn says, in spite of "some unguarded phases,"[8] Joachim did not think in such abolitionist terms when it came to sacraments, clergy, or papacy), there is no dispute that Joachim thought that he was on the verge of the new age, nor that Dante shares this conviction with him.

Another thing that is central to Joachim and also to Dante is a mind-set which interprets Christianity and indeed the world at large through the stock of its symbols. For Joachim, literalism was the enemy to men of God; much as one might see Islamic fascism, and any other kind of fascism, as built around an inflexible and merciless authority projected onto words uttered in one time and one place and arranged sequentially for a task at hand, which barely bears repetition. As Bernard McGinn says: "For the abbot of Fiore the list of history's villains is nothing else than the sum total of literalist exegesis."[9] To understand God's word means that the imagination must grasp the rich array of resemblances which are as common to words as things, and which point to the creative fecundity of the divine. This way of seeing reality, which is so intrinsic to Dante, was common enough in his age and not a peculiarity of his or Joachim's. Dante's fourfold distinction between the symbolic, the analogical, the allegorical, and the moral meaning of things, again a common enough method for his time, is at the heart of the *Comedy* thus making its cluster of elements so dynamic and multilayered, and, indeed, rendering the text incapable of interpretative exhaustion.

Possibly, Gertrude Leigh goes too far in her interpretations of Joachim and Dante by making them prophets of a spiritualized church-less world, but her very title *The Passing of Beatrice* when seen in the context of her book's thesis about Dante's heterodoxy, brilliantly encapsulates the point that Dante's majestic poetic and prophetic move rests upon his immortalizing of Beatrice after her death. At the heart of that move is his substitution of the miracle of her existence for the miracle at the center of the church's daily practice, the miracle of the Eucharist. Before the *Comedy*, Dante had written of his entrance into a *New Life*, a life made possible by the life and death of her who brings beatitude, Beatrice, a girl/young woman whose birth and death are accompanied by symbolic portents. In making so much of Beatrice, Dante puts his faith to the test—for had there been no palpable result, would Dante have not been just someone caught in the delirium of his own fantasy? The proof must lie in the deed. And Dante's proof was not only the production of the *Comedy* but its reception. Beatrice is the miracle that gave Dante his life, that made it his fate to be the poet of the Italian language, and to be able to sing of hell, purgatory, and heaven opening up the possibility (not taken, obviously) of the nations of the world transforming their existence from their living hells and purgatories to paradise. Beatrice would, through Dante, be the benefactor to all humanity, had humanity the eyes and ears to see and hear. Dante and Beatrice form an immortal couple. That is, a couple in which each has been immortalized by the existence of the other: Dante has successfully sung her name so that every day of every year someone will read of his praise and her glory; and he can only do this because she touched him in an immortal way. This, then, is not just a love that aims for "forever," but (so far at least) continues "forever," into the death of both. It is heaven sent: divine.

In *The New Life*, the God of Love leaves us midway through the poem, having said that Beatrice is to be called Love because of her great resemblance to Him. It is, as Charles Singleton says in his delightful little book *An Essay on The Vita Nuova*:

> something like a last will, delegating to Beatrice henceforth all the authority of Love. No longer will the sign of the power of a passion be other than the object and agent itself of that passion. Love, the conception of Love, is undergoing a change. Anyone who is capable of looking subtly at the matter will see now that Love is Beatrice. By such a pronouncement the God of Love might also be said to have removed himself from the stage. By his own words, he is surplus.[10]

Whether the connection is direct or not, does not change the fact that the relationship between love, beauty, goodness, and divinity is essentially the (neo-)Platonic understanding of love's purpose. In the third *Ennead*, Plotinus puts it succinctly: "Now everyone recognizes that the emotional state for which we make this 'Love' responsible rises in souls aspiring to be knit in the closest union with some beautiful object."[11] And, for Plotinus, the soul longs for beauty because the harmony, balance, and sense of perfection that characterizes beauty is itself good, is something that suggests the Good itself, which, in Plotinus, is God itself. The Christian neo-Platonism of (pseudo-) Dionysius the Areopagite (whom Dante places among the great theologians in the heaven of the Sun, and whose arrangement of the celestial hierarchy is taken over by Dante) continues the tradition.[12] The troubadours' elevation of the beloved, if not derived from neo-Platonism, was at the very least consistent with its divinization of beauty, each having made of his lady the incarnation of beauty itself. Dante continues this neo-Platonist/troubadour move, but then he makes of Beatrice the miracle that is right for the new dawn. Christ no longer speaks directly to the time in the way that the beloved Beatrice can. It is not that Christianity has become irrelevant. On the contrary, Dante believes that the new age of peace could not have been achieved without Christianity. In the *Comedy*, he has all the great pre-Christian philosophers and poets live in limbo (the pagan Elysian fields), including his guide through hell and purgatory, Virgil. In one of the *Comedy*'s most poignant moments, Virgil, humbly bends his head to acknowledge the deficiency in a way of being in the world which seeks to make sense of everything through reason alone, and that does not participate in the potency of the contingency of the cross. For Dante, the act of dying on the cross as the consummation of the life of Christ triggered a plethora of subsequent acts and orientations, more specifically the kinds of faith, hope, and love which Dante sees as essential for completing the pagan wisdom. The Christian and the pagan, for Dante, again in a gesture that is to become identified with humanism, are not enemies; though he adds, Christianity complements and fulfils what is greatest within paganism. While Christ and his disciples have demonstrated the miraculous potency of faith, hope, and love that power only creates goodness when it is combined with wisdom, temperance, justice, and courage (the classical virtues). Even Christ himself, for Dante, is a complement to Rome. For Dante, the possibility of the great peace lies in the establishment of an order just and mighty, one capable of unifying all men and women thereby putting an end to any potentially politically divisive body of men. Such an order, for Dante, was Rome. And in his *De Monarchia*, he argues that unlike other empires, Rome, which straddled Europe, Asia, and Africa, that is the entire known world, was divinely sanctioned (his reasons include Christ having been born in the empire, its durability and might, the ability of its people to put their self-interest aside "in order to promote the public interest for the salvation of mankind").[13] In the *Comedy*, he has one Trojan, Ripheus, Rome's founder as well as one pagan Roman emperor, Trajan (who myth has it, had been allowed by God to return to earth to be baptized) dwell in heaven (another Roman, Cato, is found on the shores of Purgatory). It is, then, Rome plus Christ that makes a new imperium possible, but only if the Pope gives up all political claims, and all laws and all political operations come under the rulership of the Holy Roman emperor. Throughout the *Comedy* this topic is broached again and again, as he expresses his disappointment in weak emperors and his hopes for the present and future emperors.

While Dante acknowledges the worldly change brought about through Christ's existence, and while his political vision is of a Rome Christianized, the historical personage of Christ does not suffice to slake his love. And given the corruption of the age whose wreckage Dante sees all around him, one must ask whether it sufficed to reach anyone. If we bear this in mind, then it is perhaps not surprising that in the greatest Christian love poem, Christ as a historical person never appears. There are three (the number that symbolizes the miraculous) references to him under the symbolic forms of griffin, martyr, and victor, and hence as the principles of spiritual order, spiritual victory, and universal redemption.[14] Beatrice on the other hand is both person and allegory. That she is already dead when Dante is spurred to his greatest deed by her love is precisely what severs what we may call the transcendent romanticism of Dante from the imminent faith in romantic relationships of our time. We moderns watch over and over as love withers and becomes decrepit. We want the love in its divine form actualized and sexualized. For Dante, on the other hand, its divinity lay in its actuality and beyondness. Beatrice had existed on earth and he did see her: she was real. But she was dead and was still alive in his every breath and action. They never had sex, lived together, nor squabbled. These lacks or absences were precisely the powers that fed Dante and which he drew upon to fire his imagination and heart as well as those of others.

The *Comedy* is both an accumulation of the symbols and teachings of more than a thousand years of historical Christianity and its point of creative dissolution. And just as love is at the center of the real teaching and meaning of Christianity, it is love that is at the center of the *Comedy* itself, as is evident from Virgil's remarks:

> Neither creator, nor creature was ever
>
> …my son, without love,
>
> Either natural or rational…
>
> Natural love is always without error,
>
> But the other kind may err, in the wrong object,
>
> Or else through too little vigour.
>
> While it keeps to the primal good,
>
> And keeps to its limits in relation to the secondary,
>
> It cannot be the occasion of sinful pleasure
>
> So you can understand that love must be
>
> The seed of every virtue that is in you
>
> And of every action deserving of punishment. (Purgatory XVII, 91–105)

The *Comedy* is the precise application of this principle. Thus, over the gates of hell, Dante says we find engraved: "I was the invention of the power of God, Of his wisdom, and of his primal love." Moreover, in the intricate and carefully plotted layers of hell, purgatory, and heaven, Dante presents the most artful construction of the fit between the soul's love and its own making.[15] That is to say each layer of hell, purgatory, and heaven precisely mirrors the love and motivation of the soul. The worlds of our own time and the time to come are thus our soul's writ large. That the individual is a historical being means that he or she is condemned to the sins of previous generations as well as the sins of his contemporaries. His or her only hope in the worst of times lies in the world to come. Neighborly love—and the justice that flows from that love (and in Dante justice is secondary to love)—is ultimately the difference between heaven and hell. Moreover, just as Augustine had created the polarity between God as the source of creation and the self as the receiver of God's love, Dante depicts hell as the various modalities of the soul's own appetitive enclosures—hell is for the selfish; heaven for the selfless, i.e., those whose selves become divinized through their surrender to a love that is more than themselves. In hell, on the other hand, our "sins" of omission and commission all revolve around a selfish approach to life, an approach which would steal and rip and tear apart to get at what the self thinks will satiate it, but which only brings about its own stagnation and demise. Hell is a place of self-pity, coldness, immobility (or what, for Dante, is the same, driftless/endlessly meaningless repetitious mobility) dissatisfaction and torment. It is violent and violating (selfish) love, and it is where desire goes when it does not love aright.

In sum, then, for Dante, love finds itself in nature, wisdom, justice, the universal empire of hope, the afterlife, and between man and woman. Beatrice is the hybrid of the neo-Platonist One and the troubadour's Venus. Venus returned, but subordinate to the One. Beatrice the symbol for the One, who herself must dissolve. Of course, that neo-Platonism is Christianized so that there is difference in the unity, so that Dante's mystic vision retains the distance between God and the individual soul.

Notes

1. See Charles S. Singleton, *An Essay on the Vita Nuova* (Cambridge, MA: Harvard University Press, 1958), 63–68.
2. Dante, *The Divine Comedy, Paradiso* 1, 103–26. All citations in this chapter come from Allen Mandelbaum's three-volume translation with the University of California Press, Berkeley (1980 and 1982).
3. Karl Vossler, *Medieval Culture: An Introduction to Dante and His Times*, trans. William Lawton, vol. 1 (New York: Frederick Ungar, 1958), 302.
4. *Purgatorio*, cantos III and IV.
5. See *Paradiso*, canto XII, 140–41.
6. Gertrude Leigh, *The Passing of Beatrice: A Study in the Heterodoxy of Dante* (London: Faber and Faber, 1932), chap. 2. But according to Margaret Reeves, perhaps the most well-known Joachim scholar in English, "He was favoured by four popes, yet denounced by the Cistercian Order as a runaway.... His sanctity guarded his personal reputation when his views on the Trinity were condemned in 1215, yet after 'the horrible scandal' of 1255 the Commission

of Anagni set up by the pope to examine his works condemned the whole 'fundamentum doctrine.'" Margaret Reeves, *The Influence of Prophecy in the Later Middle Ages: A Study in Joachism*, (Oxford: Clarendon, 1969), 3. In real life, Joachim was opposed by Bonventura, but in Dante's heaven Bonventura acclaims him. In the twentieth century, the political theorist Eric Voegelin argued in his *The New Science of Politics* that Joachim was largely responsible for promoting the Gnostic heresy of bringing heaven to earth which Voegelin sees as the spiritual pathology at the root of the ideological nightmares of the twentieth century.

7. Stephen Wessley, *Joachim of Fiore and Monastic Reform* (New York: Peter Lang, 1990), 46.
8. Leigh's position is at the basis of her study *The Passing of Beatrice*. For Bernard McGinn, see his *The Calabrian Abbot: Joachim of Fiore and the History of Western Thought* (New York: Macmillan, 1985), 192.
9. McGinn, *Calabrian Abbot*, 126.
10. Singleton, *Essay on the Vita Nuova*, 57.
11. Plotinus, *Ennead 3.5.1*, trans. Stephen MacKenna.
12. St. Thomas in *Paradiso* X, 115–17, is referring to his *Celestial Hierarchy*.
13. Dante, *On World Government (De Monarchia)*, trans. Herbert Schneider, introduction by Dino Bigongiari (Indianapolis, IN: Bobbs-Merril, 1949), bk. 2, sec. 5.
14. Vossler, *Medieval Culture*, 212.
15. For a more detailed account of the "logic" of heaven, purgatory, and hell, see my "The Power of Love in Dante's The Divine Comedy," in *Great Ideas in the Western Literary Canon*, ed. Wayne Cristaudo and Peter Poiana (Lanham, MD: University Press of America, 2003), 37–60.

6

Love in the Family and Its Dissolution

After Dante there is only one institutional Christian type left. That is the Christian of the reformer embodied most completely in Luther.[1] The entire basis of his defiance of Rome is the intolerable practices of the church already identified and systematically attacked by Dante. With Luther these crimes against the spirit—simony, indulgences, church corruption through its politicization—all force the Christian away from the mysterious powers claimed by the church and back into the everyday world. Luther not only teaches that every Christian is a priest, and hence the priest is not privileged above any Christian whose heart is open to God's word, but that divine service consists in being embedded in the community. The basis of that embeddedness in community is now the family. This is what Hegel grasped with such clarity. Hegel called himself a Lutheran because he saw Luther and all moderns as shaped and empowered and in service to the spirit of freedom. Freedom as the Holy Spirit, is the Spirit no longer subordinate to the Son, but now is the primary force of the Western understanding of the divine. Just as Paul had grasped that Jesus, not Yahweh, for him simply designated as the Father, was the primary spiritual power through whom the divine voice spoke and created, so Hegel *grasped* that the spiritual significance of Luther was that he had made the living presence of the spirit the truth of God's word (a particularly appropriate term for the philosopher of the *Begriff*—*Begriff* being the German for concept. But in the German, *Begriff* is derived from *begreifen*, to grasp: the tangible/graspable if one but has the hand, has the attunement, presence of the divine spirit). With Luther the Holy Spirit is in the world. And we must participate in the world for our service to be meaningful, for us to live in the truth of the spirit. When Hegel makes the family the basis of the ethical life, he is not only realizing the truth about the ethical foundation of the modern being

111

in the family, but he is following Luther in realizing that the family is the ground of the spirit in the community: it gives the primary shape in which we are tested/purified/move out into creation as whole or damaged by spirit.

The family and tribe are humanity's oldest and most enduring institutions. Once tribes reach a certain scale of complexity, they themselves adopt more complex administrative forms, lest they perish from their own internal antagonisms, squabbling, and vengeful families. They become states, although the needs of the tribe are never completely satisfied by the state and hence tribal surrogates and variants constantly appear. This is clearly evident in the residual tribal subsets of Greek and Roman states and in modern subcultures, where tribes become largely voluntary affairs (of course, the wills of its members are frequently directed by common circumstances and contingencies). Baudelaire had already recognized this need in his observation of and involvement with the dandy.

But it is not only the state that emerges out of tribal life, but in all likelihood, the family. In this respect I follow Rosenstock-Huessy who has made the interesting conjecture that the family evolves out of the tribe, and not the other way around as several political anthropologists since Aristotle had commonly held. The family, he claimed, was based upon the tribal decision to provide protection for its most vulnerable: fathers would forgo the right (the right of might) to sleep with their daughters. Certainly, the complex rites concerning sexual congress in tribal societies would seem to support the idea that the demarcation of legitimate spheres of sexual congress was closely allied with familial formations. Plato's great scandal in the *Republic*, soundly rebuked by Aristotle (and held by Allan Bloom, in his highly contentious, but no less interesting interpretative essay on that work, to be nothing more than a provocative joke exposing the absurdity of utopian thinking) was to smash to bits all familial ties. What, of course, has separated ancient and even medieval conceptions of the family from the modern version was what underpinned the motivation of the family. Apart from the possibility of acting as a protective unit, as Rosenstock suggests, it was also an economic unit. As Aristotle reminded his readers economics is about household management (the home being the *oikos*). The family was, then, primarily a means for stabilizing (and expanding) property and the accompanying domestic production. The difference between ancient and medieval marriages and modern marriages is fully conspicuous in the dowry. That parents of the daughter often pay for marriage is a remnant of the past, but it is now little more than a gesture often waived. The family then was a means for maintaining the perpetuity of a blood group. It seems that by the time of Augustus it was not that uncommon for Roman men to love their wives, and even to swear fidelity to each other. But such sentiments evolved out of the institution: they were not its source. Of course, this is precisely the opposite of what now happens in modern Western industrial societies, and why the institution is in such trouble there. Hegel's discussion of the family in his *Philosophy of Right* correctly grasped that the principle of the individual decision was something which could not be taken out of the modern world. His comments about the role of men and women (the feminine as receptive energy) was the common prejudice of philosophical minds (from Rousseau through to Kant as well as Hegel himself) impeding his grasp of the disintegrative speed of the modern, which would grab as much a hold of women as men, and ultimately bring into question almost the entire basis of the family. Friedrich Schlegel's *Lucinde*, with its case for the irrelevance of marriage where there is passionate love, a work vehemently criticized by Hegel, was far more attuned to the direction of the modern spirit than Hegel's Aristotelian rationalization of the family's centrality to the ethical life. What Hegel had done, and what all those who defend the ethical primacy of the family continually do is repeat the great Aristotelian flaw of the division of contingent things into substance and accident. From this position, defective families, i.e., families that are sites of damage and evil are accidents, whereas families that work are those in accord with their essence. Hence the family that is good is by definition true to its nature. Where families are good there can be little argument that it is a valuable institution. And all Aristotelian-derived examinations of forms gain their power from the examination of well-functioning systems. The vitality of a group of souls, which is what a group soul is, and which as a historical body gives it a mightier weight and shape than any of the individuals constituting it, is always a compelling force. But where families are not functioning, all the talk in the world about familial integrity is irrelevant. Once sexual desire became the basis for the family (for every family), it had already undergone such a metamorphosis that its demise was inevitable—as is all too obvious today by the multiformed nature of the family being built primarily around the volition of those wanting to have one.

Shakespeare's *Romeo and Juliet* provides a compellingly powerful observation of the collision course between the fragility and fickleness of the individual's will and the sturdiness of families. Insofar as his corpus constantly contrasts loving service with selfishness and pride, he is a thoroughly Christian playwright dedicated to ever reminding of the Christian alternative to tragedy. In *Romeo and Juliet*, Shakespeare brings out the difference between the love that is required to build up a family and romantic passion. In the first instance, romantic passion is simultaneously not constant yet capable of a doggedness that can result in death. Thus, Romeo who will die for love of someone he cannot live without is first seen swooning with love for someone else.

In his typical use of the "foil," the original object of Romeo's affections, Rosaline, and Paris, Juliet's suitor, unlike Romeo and Juliet, act in accordance with the weights and obligations of social circumstances—Rosaline by not succumbing to Romeo's entreaties, Paris by waiting as requested by Juliet's parents. Neither is swept away by their own passion and they do not sweep others away or drag them into their tempests. Yet they—like everybody else—are vulnerable to the tempestuousness of romantic passion, as is most evident in Paris's death at Romeo's hands. That death, of course, results from the secrecy of the love, as do the deaths of Mercutio and Tybalt. That is to say, a love that has no social seal and which must be hid completely confuses the meanings of social intentions and obligations. This is not because souls are not entitled to being veiled at times—but that marriage is a public event. And thus a secret marriage is no marriage—something spelled out in real life between Heloise and Abélard. We moderns tend to think of romance as *the* vital ingredient in marriage. Shakespeare's *Romeo and Juliette*—and indeed the world of which he is a part (not to mention all the other worlds of past and present which arrange marriages)—shows otherwise. The virtues required for marriage are patience and obligation—romantic love has no time for these virtues. Indeed, romantic love wants to storm the gates of time, those gates which make separation from the beloved unbearable, and which would transform passion into the more durable form of constancy. A marriage is a decision to join against the vicissitudes of daily life and time. It is a form of bondage—and in *The Tempest*, Shakespeare's most philosophical exposition of the complexity and character of social obligations, Miranda and Ferdinand's love is spoken of precisely in terms of bondage. Their love has been "manipulated" by Prospero's magic and this neither diminishes it nor makes it less worthy. This is because their love is ultimately not for them, but for those who have need of them. Prospero had learnt that putting his wants first—even when they included the classical virtue of pursuit of wisdom—had destroyed a dukedom, had enslaved his people and risked not only his life but that of his daughter's. He has learnt on his island the true meaning of sacrificial love, that love is not sacrificial in the sense of scapegoating—that is the avoidance of self-sacrifice by the finding of another to be the sacrifice—but in the sense of following needs that have greater importance than our own. Ultimately, we should seek to do God's will and His work, and this is why we exist. Importance itself, then, only makes sense in terms of the range and scale of the obligations and sacrifices required in doing God's work. Thus, from this point of view, the more social power one has the more responsibility one has. This is not an ideal but a simple fact of the meaning of office within Christendom, a fact, which, nevertheless was all too frequently denied by the powerful, who saw the accumulation of power as the accumulation of privilege and acquisitive opportunity.

When Locke had written his theoretical grounding of the modern representative state, *The Second Treatise of Government*, the Christian view of the meaning of life seemed completely irrelevant, and the Bible simply seemed to him to contain lessons concerning political obligation, whereas society itself seemed to have existed simply to facilitate more peaceful and improved means for developing one's property. The English civil war had shown Locke that whoever ruled would rule for acquisitive purposes—the issue was whether the acquisition was cooperative, rational, and to the benefit of the members of the commonwealth, or whether it was the rapacious act of a sovereign without responsibility. That is to say, the very prospects of Christian governance no longer even entered his field of visibility.

The Christian view of society conceives us all as potentially loving and hence suffering servants of each other. There is no love without giving, and, at times, what has to be given is the giving up of our own desire. Many scholars have labored lovingly over the ostensibly Christian source of Locke's theory of natural law, but the contradiction between the view of social purpose as personal acquisitiveness and loving servitude is absolute. The Christian view is truly sacrificial in the sublime and nonphantasmic sense—it is not identical with merely giving up one's desire as the ascetic does, for such a giving up may be done for the most selfish (and socially useless) of reasons, as Erasmus, Luther, and the reformers rightly claimed in their attack upon monasticism.

Romeo and Juliet will give up their lives for their love, but will not allow love to be a condition of growing life, which is love's real aim. Insofar as the family serves that aim it is blessed. But families are not always blessed. Again Shakespeare knew this, and his plays offer a rich account of damaged families—families plagued, inter alia, by jealousy, greed and murderous ambition, incest, parental careless indifference, ungrateful and patricidal children, revenge, and stupid pride. The family can carry the seal of love, but where love is absent it usually carries the seal of evil. When a family is healthy love comes in and out, much as air for the lungs but where violent passions circulate, it is a hothouse, closing out many of the other elements of the social world, which may nourish those damaged and desperately in need for health in a sick family.

If Romeo and Juliet is a study of tempestuous selfish love, it is also a study of tempestuous, selfish parents and kin, too caught up in their past to create a future. The deployment of marriage to create peace between warring parties is an ancient wisdom that Shakespeare fully grasps—and it is the motivation behind Friar Lawrence's decision to marry the young lovers (an ambition ruined, however, by secrecy and undue haste). If warring parties cannot be united in celebration of love, then they may be united in the mutuality of their grief—which is the final lesson of the tragedy.

Just as we all belong to bodies larger than ourselves, it is Romeo's and Juliet's misfortune to belong to warring bodies, to be but members of warring families. That fact is sealed by their names. And Juliet would unseal it by looking beyond the name. Unfortunately the longings of the heart do not automatically supply perspicacity, especially to those who lack experience. Juliet's request that Romeo "doff thy name" is as naïve as Romeo's response "I'll be new baptized." It is naïve because rebaptism is impossible—a name is a signifier of things past and future expectation.[2] A new name can only come with a new sacrament or new title bestowed from a higher authority. A new name means a new trial, a victory which carries the victories beyond the burdens of the past—burdens invariably historically registered and named. The loathsome obstacle of an ill reputed name is a challenge to be overcome through labor and time, and love's right application (but is that not the central theme of the play?). Juliette and Romeo do not know this—how could they? They are children, and this is also evident in their childish wish that lived processes simply receive new names because it suits them (a childishness too often repeated by philosophers who would suggest that names are arbitrary—their lettering might be arbitrary, but the name is a test and trial which becomes a history, a tangible weight, which is of the essence of a thing/event).

Those who watch Romeo and Juliet have the opportunity to learn the lesson that escaped the two dead lovers, viz. that our life is no more our own than our love—though we are a part of our life as we are part of our love, but not sovereign. Again the distinction between this way of seeing things and the modern is decisive—the modern emphasis upon the sovereignty of the self is from this other perspective a deluded fantasy. And Shakespeare is such a telling diagnostician of the pathologies of the modern soul because he was so alert to and horrified by the new ideas of self and world that would undergird modernity and that were just beginning to take wing in his time.

I said above that Shakespeare is all too aware of the pathologies to which families succumb, thus he does not succumb to the fantasy so frequently promulgated by Hollywood that the family (along with romance) is the key to salvation. That the family and marriage went from being something that was seen as a tolerable second best in St. Paul to an important component of loving service in the reformist view of Christianity was a healthy corrective to ascetic morbidities and unnatural excesses within Christendom. Within that context, romance could not be the basis and *telos* of the institution if it were to remain embedded in Christendom: the family, like one's profession, had to be placed in service to God; it nurtured its members so that they would be ready to respond to the call. Thus, John Milton passionately and authentically made the case in biblical terms that, in some instances, divorce was a spiritual necessity that was bound up with the following of one's calling.

The fact that the Reformation saw family life as more godly than monastic life does not change the fact of the widespread dangers to the spirit that the family may carry to generations. This is a major theme of Dostoevsky's *The Brothers Karamazov*. This majestic analysis of the intergenerational damage that has been done through family failure is an astute observation of the swirling demonic energies that brew in dysfunctional families. Fyodor Karamazov not only abandons his children, breaches sexual demarcations by pursuing the same lover as his son, he is also a rapist. No wonder that he is hated by all his sons, and murdered by his (more than likely) illegitimate son. All the Karamazov children are damaged. But it is not only they. The entire generation of young adults is damaged—thus leading Dostoevsky to cast his eyes to the next generation in the grand hope that they might be saved and become Russia's saviors. All the young women in *The Brothers* are just as psychologically deformed as the young men. Gruschenka is defiled as a young woman/girl then tossed aside because the society provides no real spiritual home for young women like her. Her sexual charisma is a curse: her playing off of Fyodor against Dymitri, her wild flirtations, and her designs on Alyosha are all sado-masochistic emotional acts that are as self-mutilating as they are harmful to others. Katarina is a manipulative hysteric, whose obsessive love for Dymitri is characterized by its absolute lovelessness and her emotionally sado-masochistic relationship with Ivan. And perhaps most sad of all is little Lisa Kholkakov. This sickly butter-wouldn't-melt-in-her-mouth young girl dreams of watching a boy being nailed to the wall and tortured as she eats pineapples while awaiting an admirer.

The cornerstone of the speeches for the prosecution and defense in Dymitri's trial all gravitate around the degeneracy of the Russian family and the failure of one generation in its provision for the next. For Dostoevsky, only the most radical spiritual solution can solve the problem that has taken hold of the Russian soul: the transformation of the state into the church, a society that follows the loving and all-embracing doctrine of the elder Zosima. Dostoevsky's solution is a leaping back and leaping forward—a desperate attempt to prevent the bloodbath he foresaw coming from the relentless pursuit of justice by the intellectuals and the faith in a Man-god. The type he feared would take over Russia was the atheistic opportunist, the man who believed in nothing but his own advancement, exemplified in the character Rakitin, the most despicable character in the entire novel. Of course his solution is an impossible one, but we admire Dostoevsky today because of his diagnoses of what was wrong with the selfishness and abstract dreams of the modern soul, not his mad pan-Slavic xenophobic rants spiced with reminiscences of saintly orthodoxy.

The modern elevation of autonomy and choice has made the family itself something to be assessed on the basis of how it nourishes the self in its projects. The persistent perception of its failure to do so has meant that the bonds at its foundation—the bond between husband and wife—are utterly precarious. What had been a union for perpetuity and property has with the widespread triumph of the myth of romance become a union based upon the need for the sublime. And none saw this more sharply than Gustave Flaubert whose *Madame Bovary* is the masterly exploration of the delusory and destructive character of the modern myth of romantic love as a quest for the sublime. In Emma Bovary we find one of the most pitiful, selfish and, yet, genuinely tragic characters in literature (to be tragic, as Aristotle insisted there must be some nobility of character whose demise we may mourn). She wants so much from life and finds instead disappointment at every turn: the disappointment of a stolidly faithful, boring, myopic, and dull-witted husband; the disappointment of a philandering cad who talks the language of sublimity, but whose real longing does not go beyond sex; the disappointment of a poetic, but ultimately bland, timid lover who could only really look attractive to someone who has almost been bored to death by her circumstance. The great survivor of *Madame Bovary*, of course, is the pseudoscientific, pseudo-Enlightened gas-bagging pseudofraternal secularist, Homais. Just as he cheerfully outlives the woman who has been driven from life by the mismatch of the possibilities reality may offer, and her impossible desires, Flaubert prophesizes that his creepily self-satisfied myth of progress will eventually eclipse Emma's myth of romance: for all societies are means for the enhancement of one type over another. But Flaubert instructs his reader that Homais's myth will be the complete and absolute triumph of boredom—that same boredom which Baudelaire had placed his finger on as the source of the modern mal-(evil)-ady. Homais is Nietzsche's blinking last man, oblivious to his own repulsiveness, and the barrenness of the world he has made.[3]

The flat earth plains of Homais which reduce the powers that had to be harnessed for science to take its place in the world of snake-oil remedies and pseudoscientific chatter, which reduce the momentous and terrifying revolutionary forces of the foundation of the modern state to blithe fraternalistic homilies (whence, of course, his name), are contrasted with the highest and lowest dimensions of hunger that make up Emma's soul. The scale of intensity is what is remarkable about Emma, and this cannot be denied no matter how self-indulgent and pathetic she becomes. Emma's "problem" is that the heights she really longs for are divine heights. And just as she has had her head full of romance while a girl in a convent, she fantasizes about a monastic life where she could engage once and for all in the divine romance. Flaubert deftly touches the nerve of the modern myth of romance: that it is first and foremost a religious myth, but it now floats free of the religious context which gave it its potency, and the passions that Emma has cannot be quenched by another human being. We recall that for Dante, even Beatrice must step aside in light of the great One. What hope has the modern family with Madame Bovary, with a woman nourished on the fantasy of romance, as a mother? The rich imagination and insatiable hunger of Emma has as its earthly correlate not only her sad and pathetic husband, but a child whose existence is but a passing shadow in Emma's grand theatrics. We do not learn what will become of that child—though one can hazard that she will be every bit as tortured as her mother, and the source of her torment will be the selfishness that disabled a mother from passing on the love that is the condition of the health of an infant's soul.

But it is not Flaubert who most caustically provides an autopsy of the modern family. This sad honor goes to Franz Kafka. His *Metamorphosis* shows that the modern family is the source of utter dehumanization. Gregor Samsa awakens to a reality in which he has become vermin, but as the story unfolds (and as Nabokov in his marvelous lecture on *Metamorphosis* so neatly observes) it is the rest of the family who show themselves to have souls of vermin. Kafka powerfully portrays the sacrificial nature of relationships through Gregor's unconditional love as he is transformed from family provider to family burden (as large vermin) who eventually chooses to die rather than interrupt the new-found energies and possibilities that have been open to them by their own greater responsibility in the world once they have kept the vermin son packed away in his room with all the other junk. The father pelting apples at his vermin son encapsulates the nightmare that takes place in so many families. The pathologies of the family will become a central source of social criticism in the 1960s culminating with R. D. Laing's identification of the connection between psychosis and family. The impact of the change in attitude from Luther can theoretically perhaps best be gauged by Jacques Derrida in *Glas*, the text of which is split into scraps/reflections/probes/flashes into, upon, about and citations from Hegel on love, family, religion—in sum: order—on the one side, and the imprisoned, homosexual, thief Genet (he who cannot in reality or dream be contained by the world into which he is born except through incarceration/execution).

Hegel is an institutionalist through and through because an institution is the collective form in which a particular aspect of life is cultivated; even when that cultivation is inefficient, is damaged or broken down in some way, our powers are only genuinely developed in our relationship with others in bodies of time. He is as determined to show that we are just as severed from our own freedom if we are not members of a family as if we are not members of a state. The young Hegel had written interesting and insightful essays on love and Christianity, but as his own philosophy developed, he did the most philosophical of things—he opted for the importance of wisdom over love. And thus his apologetics for the family, civil society, and the state—what he calls the three spheres of the ethical life—are based upon what he sees as their intrinsic rationality. For Hegel, our institutions are the ways in which our lives take on a concrete manner of freedom—they provide our lives with a positive content. Freedom, which is not accompanied, for Hegel, by a role and the accompanying responsibilities and powers commensurate with it, is empty and abstract. Like Aristotle, and for all the dynamism of the dialectic, Hegel emphasizes the benefits of stability, of routine, role, and placement. And in this respect he tries to "normalize" love within life. The problem, as we have suggested, is that when concrete families are poisonous this appeal to the ethical life no longer has much meaning or value to those living in their enclosed hells. And what is true of the family is true of every social body.

When men and women feel that what should be the source of their cultivation is, in fact, the source of their asphyxiation—they rebel. This was precisely what motivated the generation to which Marx and Kierkegaard belonged. Both sought spiritual sustenance in the poles that Hegel absolutely denied: the one a completely communal (read totalized) future without property, law, state, the family, etc.; the other in the complete individual. Kierkegaard's decision that he could not marry Regina Olsen shows, from a Hegelian point of view, the pathetic nature of the state of mind that sees its world thus.[4] Kierkegaard is the protestant who rejects the very ground of Protestantism. His private religion is, from Hegel's perspective, sheer madness, and that madness is everywhere in Kierkegaard's system. Kierkegaard is not a man but a collection of masks. But the problem with thinkers like Hegel (and Aristotle and Confucius) is that they do not understand sickness—Kierkegaard tackles this head on in a work appropriately called *Sickness unto Death*. Sickness, like the remnant, the broken thing, weakness, is the chink that lets something more powerful in.

From the Hegelian point of view lack of wholeness is associated with the unhappy consciousness, the divided consciousness, what Deleuze and Guattari will call schizophrenia, which in their philosophy is a good place to be in a world that would through its excessive order destroy all animality. Deleuze's hatred of Hegel is, again if viewed under the Hegelian optic, the hatred of the delinquent, the person who lives off society but damages it. But the delinquent, of course, sees matters very differently: society is a great complex of hypocrisy, and perversion is the label given by (the bourgeois) hypocrites to the natural joys of existence which one must steal in the unnatural hell-hole of the normal.

121

The delinquent does see the truth of society, indeed s/he is the outgrowth and hence a particular embodiment of the truth of their society. And that truth is also that such a person who deforms others in their social interaction is resistant to the reforms that moralists promise to make, or perhaps, as Foucault cleverly suggests, in *Discipline and Punish*, talk of making so that the systemic (or, to use a theological term not deployed by Foucault, the demonic) recycling of power can be undertaken for the production of a class living off the sacrifice and torture of others. All delinquency is a challenge to love, for love to find a way that is all too often concealed or closed from it.

Notes

1. The Reformation by emphasizing the invisibility of spirit and teaching mistrust of visible signs thus prepared the way for what Rosenstock-Huessy has called incognito, nondenominational Christians—that they do not even want to be described thus may well be the case, and the description is to facilitate us seeing historical and spiritual continuities which we can see as undeniable. See Eugen Rosenstock-Huessy, *The Christian Future—or The Modern Mind Outrun* with an introduction by Harold Stahmer, (New York: Harper & Row 1966), 126–27. The opportunity and challenge for incognito, nondenominational Christians is to complete the Reformation by seeing suffering, serving, loving life as it is. Doing this may enable us to see the inner truth of Christian symbols and rituals which encapsulate the Christian insights into how love triumphs over death, but there are many who love and live in service to love's spirits without any knowledge or understanding of the symbolic depths and scope of the Christian tradition. The danger of that is historical deprivation and an inability to appreciate how events are large processes which radiate and shape subsequent actions.

2. The importance of names is a key idea in the works of Rosenstock-Huessy. There is a full discussion of it in the third section of his sociology, vol. 1, presently being translated by Jurgen Lawrens, and edited by myself, Francis Huessy, and Gottfried Paasch.

3. The picture of the last man in *Thus Spake Zarathustra* picks up on *The Second Untimely Meditation* where Nietzsche had screeched against the anodyne picture of spirituality that David Strauss had outlined when he insisted that the spiritual impulses which gave birth to religion had now found their free and complete forms in the bourgeois world of the theater, café, art gallery, and concert hall. For Nietzsche, the sheer indiscriminate clumping of these bourgeois "outings" was the tell-tale sign of the philistinism into which the world was sinking.

4. Kierkegaard was engaged to Regina Olsen but broke off the engagement with her. He did this because he felt that being married and having a family would lead to a life of mediocrity. It was a decision that he defended over and over again and which he, nevertheless, regretted his whole life long.

7

De Sade and the
Love of Evil

Of all delinquents, rebels, outsiders, "men in revolt," none is more revolting than de Sade, a point not lost on Camus whose book *The Rebel* (though a more literal translation would be *Man in Revolt*) makes Sade the archetypical expression of the metaphysical rebel, the rebel who wants to undo the entire cosmic order, and by so doing finds himself formulating a paradigm in which murder is rationalized, sexualized, and "massified." Baudelaire, a great admirer of the "divine marquis," as Sade came to be known, saw him as the great instructor of evil. "One must," he simply said, in a "List of titles and outlines for novels and stories," "always return to Sade to observe mankind in its natural state and to understand the quality of evil."[1] Sade did not only understand evil, he loved it. His texts, drenched as they are in sexual fluids and blood, are cries of a cosmic love. To be sure it is an inverted form of all that had usually been thought of as love—a love of murder, of rape, or torture, of horror, of ugliness, of pain, indeed of the gamut of the intoxicating cruelties of humanity in the midst of the violent sacrificial pagan carnival that Christianity had sought to eliminate. Indeed, it is because of Sade's inversions that Octavio Paz has said that "Sade was an enemy of love,"[2] and, if we conceive of love in the "normal" way he is right. In romanticized versions of love the elevation of the beloved is accompanied by an intensification of the positive personal attributes of the beloved, what Stendhal has labeled crystallization. The intoxicating power of love involves building up; in Sade, the intensification of pleasure requires belittling, tearing down, torturing, and annihilation. "[T]here is," he writes, in that matter-of-fact tone he would deploy to build his monstrous characters and scenarios, "no libertine at least a little steeped in vice who is not aware of the great sway murder exerts over the senses, and how voluptuously it determines a discharge"; "Do you still not understand that the more horror one enwraps pleasure in, the more charming she becomes?"[3]

Sexuality that does not trespass into the regions of death holds little to no interest for Sade; pornography is a preparatory step and pornography which does not lead to the more intoxicating brew of sexual murder and torture is dull and boring (consider his harsh judgment on the pornography of the novelist Restif de la Bretonne). Equally true, though, for Sade, is that death which is not accompanied by sexual intoxication is meaningless, a wasted opportunity for an intoxicating encounter at the edge of life and death. Hence the writer who justifies rape and mass murder could, in real life, be opposed to the Jacobin terror. In Sade's direct engagement with republican France "Yet Another Effort, Frenchmen, If You Would Become Republicans," in *Philosophy in the Bedroom*, he demands the elimination of all laws which have their basis in virtue addressing the deficiency of capital punishment as follows:

> because the law which attempts a man's life is impractical, unjust, inadmissible...since the law, cold and impersonal, is a total stranger to the passions which are able to justify in man the cruel act of murder. Man receives his impressions from Nature, who is able to forgive him this act; the law, on the contrary, always opposed as it is to Nature and receiving nothing from her, cannot be authorized to permit itself the same extravagances: not having the same motives, the law cannot have the same rights.[4]

The law does not satisfy, it merely utilizes Nature for something abstract. But we are of flesh and blood and other dischargeable fluid. Paz again: "the true reality was the pleasure that annihilates everything."[5] It is the annihilation, this craving for total extinction that is at the center of Sade's "love," and on a number of occasions he entertains the demise of the entire human race. It is thus also the very inversion of the Augustinian formulation of the love that would be stronger than death. Sade, of course, completely reverses the order of Augustine's hierarchy of love and eliminates God in the process so that the self is but part of the tumult of the violence of the world and God but a fantasy of a self that cannot see that the neighbor is there to be used to enhance one's own and the world's pleasure in the suffering and torment of life. And just as he inverts Augustine, he thoroughly reverses the Platonic doctrine of the ascent of eros. The more "wholesome" Plato thinks, like most "normal" people that the pursuit of sexual pleasure is bound up with the pursuit of beauty, but it is precisely the violation of beauty that is required for Sade's pleasure. "Beauty," he writes in *The 120 Days of Sodom*,

> belongs to the sphere of the simple, the ordinary, whilst ugliness is something extraordinary, and there is no question but that every ardent imagination prefers in lubricity the extraordinary to the common place. Beauty, health never strikes one save in a simple way; ugliness, degradation deal a far stouter blow, the commotion they create is much stronger, the resultant agitation must hence be more lively.[6]

While Sade argues the case for ugliness above, the defilement of the beautiful and innocence is as much part of the program, as intercourse with the ugly—thus the elaborate selection process of the beautiful children by the ugly debauched libertines in *120 Days*. The beautiful is never to remain beautiful, it must be dragged into the ugly. The real ecstasy comes when the beautiful "object" is broken, when the beauty has been extracted from the object and the monstrous within it revealed as it is set free to submit to the libertine's desires. For Sade, eros does not elevate us to the good, but rightly followed it takes us all the way down into the blood and the mud, the bone and the fire of bodies whose interlocking potentials are disclosed through brutalizing, beating, maiming, carving, and every manner of sexualized penetration.

If Sade's libidinous fantasies conjure up on a grander scale the appetitive forces and deeds of Nero and Caligula, the mechanistic metaphysical plane on which the fantasies are staged contribute to their excess both in scale and intensity. In this respect he welcomes what Alexander Koyré had called the open universe, because it is limitless in the possibilities that lie before us. However, we know that the infinite nature of the universe originally opened for the astronomers of the sixteenth century because they were originally looking at the heavens, then, as with Leibniz, attention turned to the microscopically infinite, but Sade is interested in an infinite which such men of good will, good faith, and hope all ignored—the infinite depth of eros' acquisitive insatiability.

Indeed more than anyone, the Marquis de Sade discloses the dark or demonic side to mechanistic metaphysics. Like Spinoza and Kant he accepts and defends (ceaselessly) the concept of nature as nothing other than the sum of its laws as an unbreakable chain of cause and effect. As with Spinoza, for Sade, there is no God left over and above nature, and the idea of retaining God is "a mere idea":

> [T]he universe runs itself, and the eternal laws inherent in Nature suffice, without any first cause or prime mover to produce all that is and all that we know: the perpetual movement of matter explains everything…The universe is an assemblage of unlike entities which act and react mutually and successively with and against each other.[7]

The indisputable truth of mechanism, for Sade, means that the stupid belief in a God can and must be overthrown. As with all of the doctrinal positions adopted by Sade, the following quote is just one of an endless barrage that appears throughout his books: God's commandments

> are in no wise respect-worthy; they are absurd, contrary to right reason, they are offensive to our moral sense and are physically afflicting, they who proclaim the law violate it night and day, and if indeed there is in the world a scattering of personages who seem moved to express faith in this law, let us carefully scrutinize their mentalities, we will discover them to be simple-minded or lunatic.[8]

One cannot stress enough how deeply implicated the Enlightenment of reason is in Sade's rationalizations of ecstatic mass murder. Thus, in the midst of their great chambers of hell, his characters elaborately rationalize their deeds as if they were appearing in some great cosmic law court in which the judge must come down on the side of the murderer and the torturer because the murderer and torturer is the most truthful of all human beings, truthful to nature in toto, to his or her own nature and truthful in what s/he says about nature. In other words, Sade's characters not only do evil, they are absolutely attuned to the meaning of what they do. "I'll yield to your arguments if they're logically sound" says the Count de Gernande as if he were the disinterested Socrates seeking the benign radiance of truth instead of a blood-drinking libertine.[9] Or from the same work, when Rombeau expresses concerns that he had had about Rodin's reluctance to slaughter his daughter for scientific purposes, Rodin answers:

> What! because she is my daughter? A capital reason!… what rank do you then fancy this title must allot in my heart? I place roughly the same value…upon a little semen which has hatched its chick, and upon that I am pleased to waste while enjoying myself. One has the power to take back what one has given; amongst no race

that has ever dwelled upon this earth has there been disputed the right of disposing of one's children as one sees fit. The Persians, the Medes, the Armenians, the Greeks enjoyed this right in its fullest latitude.[10]

For Sade, someone brave enough to pursue their appetites is a true child of nature, of reason, and of freedom, i.e., only the truly free human being, the libertine, is genuinely enlightened.

No doubt Spinoza would have been horrified to be cited (along with Vanini and the author of *Le Système de la Nature*) as providing the philosophical basis for Sade's apology for murder and the prosperities of vice (as the subtitle of *Juliette* reminds the reader who may not have the brains to work out its theme).[11] But it is Spinoza who first says "Desire is the actual essence of man, insofar as it is conceived, as determined to a particular activity by some given modification of itself,"[12] which is precisely how Sade sees man. Moreover, for Spinoza (again Sade follows him) desire is part of a triumvirate—pain and pleasure being the other two "primary emotions." Pleasure, for Spinoza, is "the transition of man from a less to a greater perfection" and pain "the transition of a man from a greater to a less perfection."[13] Love as well as good and evil are defined in terms of these more primary emotions, thus "Love is pleasure, accompanied by the idea of an external cause,"[14] thereby any notion of love commensurate with the pure gift of agape is simply discounted as impossible, in much the same way as his system and Descartes's world rule out any possibility of miracles. Likewise, a new moral scale is set up—one that the Sophists, and subsequently Epicureans had advanced and one that Plato had frequently refuted, viz. that "the knowledge of good and evil is nothing else but the emotions of pleasure and pain, in so far as we are conscious thereof."[15] And "by good here I mean every kind of pleasure, and all that conduces thereto, especially that which satisfies our longings, whatsoever they may be. By evil, I mean every kind of pain. Especially that which frustrates our longings."[16] Our empowerment, for Spinoza, requires the fulfillment of our nature: that fulfillment is only possible through the understanding of the power of nature as such of which we are but a part. For Spinoza, although things are but modes of one substance—God—they are destined to strive to preserve themselves and expand their own power. As a part, and like all parts we are driven beings, *conatus* or striving machines. It is this striving for persistence that enables Spinoza to reintroduce purposefulness to individual lives—and I stress the term "individual." For Spinoza provides the very modern contrast of self and totality (substance) which "drains" away the specificities of what earlier had been referred to as God's creatures.

In Spinoza's system, then, love, pleasure, good, desire all neatly line up so that our essence and our end are determined by a drive for pleasure, and the authentic self-sacrifice that is intrinsic to the Jewish and Christian form of love is but one more fantasy, one more piece of morbid imagining which distorts the truth that ethical behavior is built upon knowledge of genuine self-interest, genuine pleasure, and a genuine understanding of the laws of nature, which, in Spinoza's system, fortunately enough all work out harmoniously. It never occurs to him that his world of objects wherein each strives to preserve itself in the pursuit of its pleasure may simply be reopening a modality of rationalization in which the mimetically violent world of the pagan could again roam free. Sade, on the other hand, understood this, and embraced it.

One correlate of this is that it implies a thorough plasticity—and that plasticity persists from him to Kant to Nietzsche and Heidegger through to post-structuralism. All that is needed to ensure the benign transmogrifications of which the self is capable is knowledge of God/ nature. And Kant provides a brilliant attempt to supplement Spinoza's philosophy—but his philosophy is even more loveless than Spinoza's, working as it does with a moral philosophy in which love, as a seductive "heteronomous force," i.e., a force not generated by reason itself, *must* be banned. Whether one thinks Kant succeeds in "improving" upon Spinoza depends upon what one thinks of Kant's moral philosophy: whether it really salvages human dignity from the machine of nature, or whether it is but the vapid gas emitted from the machine. If Kant strives to salvage our dignity from the machine, Robespierre and St. Just use virtue to transform that machine into a killing machine, victims are chosen because they fail to adequately conform to virtue. "Virtue," as Robespierre so famously formulated it "is terror."

Hegel will provide one of his most brilliant dialectical analyses of the logic that leads from the originally sacrosanct nature of pleasure in the Enlightenment (Descartes's system also takes a particular kind of pleasure, namely comfort, as its end) to terror in his *Phenomenology of Spirit*. For Hegel, the "enlightenment finds it foolish when the believer gives himself the superior consciousness of not being in bondage to natural enjoyment and pleasure by actually denying himself natural enjoyment and pleasure."[17] Having denuded faith to

the barren objects and externals of ritual which symbolize powers felt
and revered and which, by their nature cannot be objects as such, the
enlightenment attack upon superstition is also an elevation of its own
consciousness: "what is for faith the absolute Being, is a Being of its
own consciousness, is its own thought."[18] That is, a key characteristic of
enlightenment thought is the elevation of human consciousness—and
although Spinoza eschews all dualism, insofar as he is forced to distinguish between cognitive mechanisms, he no less than the dualist
Descartes, and indeed like all other Enlightened thinkers, makes the
same commitment to changing the world through a fresh and cleansed
understanding of the laws of nature that take account of our natural
needs and potentials. That elevation involves both a reduction of the
world to what has utility for that consciousness and an awareness of
the power of the elevated consciousness itself. The human world is
thus the projection of a will, and all differences between peoples, differences of social position, for example, rest on nothing but the will.
Concomitantly, just as the enlightenment consciousness had seen
the God of religion as the fictional creation of the priestly class, differences between men was merely a fiction which could be overcome
by means of the right form of governance. Government itself is but
the expression of a general will. But, as Hegel rightly perceives, the
individual consciousness as it elevates itself makes of itself the general
will. Thus, Robespierre and St. Just, for example, are nothing but the
expressions of the general will; being thus they can do no wrong, being
thus all opposition to them and their way of thinking is opposition to
the good of humanity as such. The dialectic that takes one from the
search for absolute freedom and into the slaughterhouse and gulags
is magnificently summed up when Hegel writes:

> By virtue of its own abstraction, it (consciousness) divides itself
> into extremes equally abstract, into a simple, inflexible cold univer-
> sality, and into the discrete, absolute hard rigidity and self-willed
> atomism of actual self consciousness. Now that it has completed
> the destruction of the actual organization of the world, and exists
> now for itself, this is its sole object, an object that no longer has any
> content, possession, existence, or outer extension, but is merely this
> knowledge of itself as an absolutely pure and free individual self. All
> that remains of the object by which it can be laid hold of is solely
> its abstract existence. The relation, then, of these two, since each
> exists indivisibly and absolutely for itself, and thus cannot dispose
> of a middle term which would link them together, is one of wholly
> unmediated pure negation, a negation, moreover, of the individual

as a being existing in the universal. The sole work and deed of universal freedom is therefore death, a death too which has no inner significance or filling, for what is negated is the empty point of the absolutely free self, it is thus the coldest and meanest of all deaths, with no more significance than cutting off a head of cabbage or swallowing a mouthful of water.[19]

To repeat the point, in Girardian terms, this new emancipator reasoning is a new mimetic outbreak, the justification of which is that it will enable men and women to live in comfort and/or virtue, but, in fact, is just a great construction of a new sacrificial machine. And whereas a St. Just or a Robespierre see Sade as a debauched remnant of an old decaying order who is so evil he too needs to be sacrificed; for Sade, people like St. Just and Robespierre are unnecessarily masking what is really going on—they are really erecting a huge rhetorical smokescreen of virtue so that they can enjoy the murder that produces their real erections. But under their submission to the law, they do not even realize it—they suffer from the very disease that Sade most fears (and which, of course, is the great fear of all murdering sadists)—impotence. For Sade, impotence must be defeated at all costs—his ejaculatory cry "I say unto you: Fuck! You were born to fuck. To be fucked. Nature created you."[20] It is a real libertine like Juliette who knows what she is doing, who achieves that degree of sovereignty that Maurice Blanchot sees as the real purpose of Sade, and which, as we have said, is the real fulcrum of the enlightenment itself.[21] After having indulged in an orgy where she and her lover murder his sons before murdering her own daughter, she poisons fifteen hundred townspeople, while later producing a pestilence that "carried off twenty thousand."[22] With a Juliette this is all done for no other reason than to exacerbate her pleasure. And has Juliette not simply responded to the modern dream which even precedes mechanistic metaphysics and finds its early formulation in the law of Rabelais's utopian Abbey of Thélème, "Do what you will?" That law had so clearly drawn the line between what Rabelais saw as the superstitious past of Christendom and where man needs to go if he is to follow his nature, and not cut it out as Rabelais clearly thinks is required if we but heed the prior law of Augustine, "Love God, and do what thy will" which he has merely truncated, and thus overturned.[23] Rabelais's law is formulated in stark opposition to both Catholic and sausage-eating (Protestants) fools whom he thinks are equally as stunted as each other. Rabelais may have grown out of humanism and the Reformation, but his is an early voice calling for something heretofore almost unheard of—unmitigated freedom.

Instead, then, of the various masks we adopt to pursue our real pleasure and which only serve to obstruct our desires, to thwart our nature, we would be better just to accept that impotence can be overcome through murder, that life is a line from the dead to the living—we are ingesters of the dead, and our ingestion of them is so that we can live, and this same reasoning applies to the consumption of sexual power—as we rip and tear life and energy from the victim in order to vitalize ourselves. To the extent that Robespierre and St. Just do not realize this they remain as impotent as their virtue. Seen thus the question for Sade is why and how one chooses those to be sacrificed and the real difference, then, between those who pursue total virtue and total evil is simply in who is gratified and to what pitch. Life is the embodiment of a natural demand and infinitely restless search and striving for complete satiation, for complete freedom, not only not stopping at the death of the other, but feasting feverishly off that death, literally ingesting and inhaling and imbibing the life force through the others' blood and cries and pain, life in its rawest, most bloody, cannibalistically uninhibited and—to repeat—intoxicating form. If Christianity had fathomed that we nourish each other through spiritual ingestion, Sade is the return of the pagan understanding of ingestion—the literal ingestion of blood and flesh as a means of energizing the self—and the murderer and murdered vitally peak at the moment orgasm and death become one. Sade finds and celebrates what Schelling, in the very different context of mind and nature, had called the point of indifference; Sade positions himself within the point of indifference between life and death, pleasure and pain, freedom and total subordination. Sade thus must find people to be violated, to be sacrificed so that he can live—without them he might as well be dead—for there are only two kinds of feeling for Sade: intoxication and boredom (leading to impotence). With Sade it is always his prescience that is so shocking and which is why, in spite of being a contender for the most boring novelist ever, he always fascinates and demands philosophical engagement. Baudelaire will underscore that the modern malady is boredom and that our modern means of transcendence, through sex, drugs, liquor, and stimulants such as his own poetry, is the necessary response to boredom—but he dared not go so far as Sade who suggests that the only way real satisfaction on earth can be found is through monstrous feasts of sacrificial murder.

131

In this respect, Sade is also the modern return of the ancient hunt for the sacrificial victims—the plural is important. Just as Rabelais suggests that the new way forward will involve a monstrous scale—the thing about Sade is not merely the insistence upon the intrinsically murderous nature of our desire, but that its genuine liberation requires a gargantuan staging that is equivalent to the gargantuan scale of our appetites and imagination and sense of freedom, a sense for whom only the total abyss will suffice.

Sade is thus pagan in all manner of ways and he hails the return of the pagan. Rabelais precedes him to the extent that he mourns the fact that Christianity had killed the great and ancient god Pan, but he enthusiastically welcomes him back in the new, humanist, world, traveling in the omnivorous form of Pantagruel. But Rabelais's appetitive giants have no imagination to match Sade's sexually charged mass murdering spectacles. That is to say, unlike Sade, Rabelais has no idea of what resurrecting Pan might mean in the context of a universe deprived of any sacred meaning. In this respect, Sade's is a paganism without the sacred, or perhaps better an enormous shift of the sacred from its archaic and primordial origins. That is to say, Sade embraces the return of the sacrificial pagan world in order to spread violence—but not conduct it outside of the community, but for the sake of an ever more ecstatic contagion—for the voyeur, for the spectator (does not the modern cinematic taste with its need to stimulate our jaded and dulled sensibility confirm this daily?), and for the active participant, who thanks to Sade himself, we now call the sadist, whose pleasure is feverishly intensified by the cries, shakes, and visages of pain in the victim. Thus, the victim is no longer sacralized in order to stop the spread of violence; rather the sacred is the intensification of the pleasure that is absolutely dependent upon violence. It is the self truly in tune with the cosmos, without pretense and without fear—the fear of the victim being but fuel for the murderer's desire to literally overcome fear, the fear emanating from the victim. It is the return not of the pagan community—for Sade's feverishly mad version of absolute sovereignty and absolute freedom and absolute desire renders any community impossible—it is the return of the type that Plato studied so intensely, the tyrant who simply rapes and pillages a people because his appetites are insatiable and no one can stop him.

But if Sade is calling for a violent and predatory libertine "order" of sexual ecstasy (and we note how much Sade loved to detail the number and kinds of participants and routines and times in his enormous sexual dungeons), his animosity to the community and the cold calculability of law is also based on one other fact—that to that order he is a victim. And on every page of his work, Sade is screaming "*j'accuse*." He accuses the human race of its sheer hypocrisy. Everywhere it feasts upon cruelty, from its wars, its jails, its entertainment (even more pronounced in our day than Sade's), to its religion (much of the Old Testament: one long bloody tract of murder and mayhem); hell as an excuse to feel pleasure in other's pain; consider Tertullian's and St. Thomas's claim that the pleasure of the blessed is increased by the torments of the damned). While he is condemned for presenting the most disgusting spectacles, his response is that the difference between him and what all people do is negligible. His taste is the same old cruelty with sexual spice thrown into the mix. In his attack upon Villeterque, Sade insists that he has never written an immoral book.[24] And in *Reflections on the Novel*, Sade insisted that he "had no wish to make vice seem attractive," and "never shall I portray crime other than clothed in the colors of hell. I wish people to see crime laid bare, I want them to fear it and detest it, and I know no other way to achieve this end than to paint it in all its horrors." But the truth of this can only be accurately assessed by what accompanies it, a vehement denial of the authorship of *Justine*. Those who accuse him of being the author of *Justine* are, he says, imbeciles and evildoers.

The defense contains a half-truth and blatant lie; the half-truth is that there is a kind of moralism in Sade, as I have indicated the moralism of "look at what you do. I make up stories about cruelty and torture, but I do so in the prison where torture routinely takes place." Just as Sade's philosophical stories are a ceaseless voyeuristic exploration of predatory desires and idiot victims, he is a victim of the acting out and telling of the truth. That Sade sees himself as a victim (he had engraved upon his tombstone that he was "the eternal victim" of tyranny) is central to the psychological shape of his writing (the cruel are in search of sufferers who suffer in search of the cruel). Sade affirms life as one ecstatic revelry, the revelry of jailer and jailed, of torturer and tortured, of the crowd and the condemned man. In his fantasies, and in moments of freedom, he could share that revelry from the side of the perpetrator of cruelty, but much, indeed most of his life, he was called upon to play the role of the sacrifice. The people's cruelty which was expressed in the moralism of the judges and jailers could be satisfied by Sade playing his part. What looks so shocking is that Sade feverishly embraces this role. It is impossible not to suspect that Sade saw himself as a Christ figure. But whereas Christ submits to the will of the father in heaven, Sade submits to the will of nature; whereas Christ on the cross remains a figure of devotion, Sade is at once a defiant figure accusing the world of its hypocrisy, yet Sade sees himself forgiving humanity with the kind of infinite compassion that we usually associate with Christ. And whereas Christ became the sacrifice to stop the sacrifice of the Other, Sade takes his revenge on being the sacrifice by creating the most monstrously antisocial (which is equivalent to antihypocritical) literary mimesis ever conceived. But, to repeat, he has decided not only to reproduce the entire carnival of human brutality and grotesqueness through the prism of the sexually ecstatic, but to urge for its endless expansion and repetition. He takes on the role of sacrificial victim not in order to stop people doing the cruelty they do, but to love the cruelty more and to do it for the love of the act itself rather than the artifice they drape around it—at the same time he is using his fiction to show how it should be done properly.

As we have suggested then, Sade's worldview is at once demonic, perversely Christian, and materialist. It is Christian, as we have said, doctrinally in its infinite forgiveness and surrender (perversely in what it forgives and what it surrenders to), and institutionally insofar as it is the revealed symptom of, and ferocious reaction to, almost two thousand years of the social and political triumph of bodily repression; it is demonic in its complete affirmation of our darkness and it is materialist in its insistence that nature is the truth.

In spite of Sade's frequent forays into philosophical relativism, which indicate good and evil are simply matters of nomenclature, Sade's vision of the cosmos is of nature as essentially evil and the perpetuation of evil which he advocates is simultaneously an act of complete conformity with nature and total defiance: defiance because we kill nature's creations, conformity because nature itself is always killing itself and giving birth out of itself. In spite of all his antireligious protestations, Sade's cosmic vision is a variant of the Dionysian doctrine of death and rebirth and the Manichean and Gnostic depiction of the world as presided over by an evil deity; in Sade's case nature is the evil deity, and there is no possible escape. All that awaits us is the endless transposition of material formations and configurations indifferent to our search for closure, meaning, and salvation. One might say that this makes us divine.

The idea of Sadian divinization noticed by Klossowski and Bataille is most explicitly expressed in Pauline Réage's *Story of O*, a work that is thoroughly Sadian in its psychological inspiration, though, it takes the perspective of the "victim," a masochist. The real theme of the *Story of O* is the proximity between divinity and sacrifice. For example, O explains that she is a sacrifice to her lover as she gives herself completely, in total surrender.[25] Other women, she tells us, hold part of themselves back, out of self-respect, or dignity, or desire, or self-control. It is irrelevant why people hold back; the effect is the same, viz. lack of entrance into the world where divinity and abandonment fuse into total ecstasy. The surrender of O, then, creates a double divinization, of her master and herself. "Thus" she says of her master "would he possess her as a god possessed his creature as whereupon he lays hands guised as monster or bird, as some invisible spirit or as ecstasy itself."[26] And "She was no longer free? Ah! thank God no, she wasn't any longer free. But she was buoyant, a cloud-dwelling goddess, a swift-swimming fish of the deeps, but deep-dwelling, forever doomed to happiness."[27]

In his book on Sade, Gorer rightly observes "there is very little [in Sade] which could not be paralleled in Foxe's or Wright's *Book of Martyrs*."[28] And this is thoroughly grasped by the writer of *The Story of O*, where the Christian conception of martyrdom can be clearly discerned. Though there is one very large qualification if we are talking about masochism, that it is a willing surrender to the sexual desires in which the pain experienced is an intentional trigger for pleasure.

What separates the religiousness of paganism and (some strands of Christianity) from the modern preoccupation with freedom and self-mastery is the insight that it is the disintegration and abandonment of the self that is the entrance to heaven/the underworld/the divine. In search of her divinization, O, like the yogi or mystic, conspires to erase every connection to the world but that which is part of the divine line (which, for O is a line of and through pain and pleasure). Her lover and his pleasure and her concentration upon the next ceremony preoccupy her mind; all else is distraction, irritation, merely mundane. The masochist's surrender must be as total as the freedom that the Sadian libertine insists is his natural right. And all the time she borders on the edge of death. Her salvation and her doom are thus one and the same:

> Doomed because those powerful ligatures, those hair-thin cables whose ends René held in his hand were the only lines by which life-giving energy could reach her. And that was so true when René slackened his grip upon her—or when she fancied he had—when he seemed faraway, or when he absented himself in what O took for

indifference, or when he remained some time without seeing her or answering her letters and when she thought he didn't want to see any more of her, everything came to a halt in her, she languished, she asphyxiated...Cool water made her nauseous. She felt like a pillar of salt, a statue of ash, bitter, useless and damned, like the salt statues of Gomorrah. For she was guilt ridden like a sinner. Those who love God and whom God abandons in the darkness of the night, are guilty, they are sinners because they are abandoned. What sins have they committed? They search for them in their memory of the past. ....When she'd been a child she'd read a text written in letters of red upon the white wall of the room she'd spent two months living in, in Wales: a passage from the Bible, one such as Protestants inscribe in their houses: "It is a terrible thing to fall into the hands of the living God." Every time René postponed the moment when they'd see one another...O was brought thus to bay by the wolves of madness and despair; in vain.[29]

What O draws out is the most primordial recognition of sacrifice as an essential component of the human condition, as the necessary condition for the continuation of life. It is that primordial recognition that lies behind the transformation of a cosmic fact of life's interdependency with death that then leads to the social phantasm that the sacralization of a victim will lead to a community being delivered from its plagues its sins. The phantasmic sacrificial structure understands the contagious nature of evil, but fails to understand the deliverance from evil that the gift of love provides. In this strangest of ways *The Story of O* brings the Christian understanding of love as the gift which interrupts the circuit of contagion into the most elemental energies. The Sadean element is, in this moment and context, truly divine.

A similar point though with a less theological spin is put upon the phenomenon in Jean Paulhan's essay "A Slave's Revolt: An Essay on the Story of O." This essay discusses the liberation of the imagination that takes place in sado-masochistic practice in the context of the "anonymitization" and dehumanization that accompanies modernization. Paulhan touches on the childishness of the sado-masochistic relationship, childish in the sense that the child's world is one in which imagination may dictate identity, where passions roam freer, where giggles and cries and screams are an acceptable and constant aspects of reality. At the same time, he (much like Sade) throws the cruelties of modern reality into the face of moralists, emphasizing that in spite of its self-image the scale of cruelties is grander, though at the expense of sacrificing the personal for the abstract. The paradox is that what may seem to be so dangerous is so desirable because it is a zone of safety, a zone in which so much else of life is closed out—safety in cruelty. That is part of this strange transcendence which is essential to O's character. Apart from ecstatic transcendence and abandonment there is nothing else to her character. O is in love with René, but there is no relationship outside of the master–slave relationship. But this is understandable from her point of view: nothing else matters, just as no one else matters. Slavery and freedom are the merging totalities. But where does this mergence lead? ... inevitably in *The Story of O*, and in keeping with Sade, to death. O's fate is sealed: murder or else the whole thing is mere titillation. The Augustinian formulation "love is stronger than death," the meaning of Christianity and the church, is the antithesis of Sade's and O's foundational belief that all life ends in death, and all meaning ends there. Everything else is just a potentially ecstatic occasion upon the way. But at that ecstatic moment and in O's gift love steps forward to speak, to tell us that even in the darkest dungeon and through the most degraded of souls it may make its entrance, and overturning our expectations and the more stable and predictable zones of safety, demands that we pull off our moral spectacles and look deeply into its ever transformative presence.

Notes

1. Charles Baudelaire, *Oeuvres Complètes*, (Paris: Édition de la nouvelle française, 1918), 595.
2. Octavio Paz, *An Erotic Beyond: Sade*, trans. Eliot Weinberger (New York: Harcourt Brace, 1998), 79.
3. *120 Days*, 205.
4. *Philosophy in the Bedroom* in Marquis de Sade, *Three Complete Novels: Justine. Philosophy in the Bedroom, Eugénie de Franval and Other Writings*, comp. and trans. Austryn Wainhouse and Richard Seaver with introductions by Jean Paulham and Maurice Blanchot (London: Arrow, 1965), 310.
5. Ibid.
6. *120 Days* in *The 120 Days of Sodom and Other Writings*, trans. Austryn Wainhouse, (New York: Grove, 1994), 233.
7. Marquis de Sade, *Juliette*, trans. Austryn Wainhouse (New York: Grove, 1968), 43.
8. Ibid., 41–42.
9. Ibid., 645.
10. Ibid., 552.
11. Ibid., 20.
12. Baruch Spinoza, *Ethics*, bk. 3, "Definition of Emotions," 1.
13. Ibid., II and III.
14. Ibid., VI.

15. *Ethics*, pt. IV, prop. 8.
16. *Ethics*, pt. III, prop. XXXIX, note.
17. G. W. F. Hegel, *Phenomenology of Spirit*, trans. A. V. Miller, with analysis of the text and foreword by J. N. Findlay (Oxford: Clarendon Press, 1977), 556, 595.
18. Ibid., 549.
19. Ibid., 590.
20. de Sade, *Juliette*, 84.
21. His essay "Sade" is in the Seaver and Wainhouse edition of *Justine* cited throughout this chapter.
22. de Sade, *Juliette*, 1185–92.
23. To be sure there are numerous scholars who think Rabelais a Christian humanist or Christian neo-Platonist and who point out that he was a clergyman—(on this last point how can one forget that the first overtly atheistic tract in France was also written by a cleric?) Such interpretations seem to me neither to understand Christian humanism, Christian neo-Platonism, nor Rabelais. The lay Abbey of Thélème fully fits with his relentless attacks upon all those social institutions and social parasites that he believed thwarted human appetites and thereby stunted human growth. For a fuller, though brief account of Rabelais, see my essay on him, "Rabelais' Vitalism OR Feasting, Flagons, Fornicating, Fighting, Fertility, Farting, Fun and Freedom from Fear and Fools in *Gargantua and Pantagruel*," in *Great Ideas in the Western Literary Canon*, with Peter Poiana.
24. *120 Days*, 122.
25. Pauline Réage, *The Story of O* (London: Corgi, 1972), 28.
26. Ibid., 27.
27. Ibid., 77.
28. Geoffrey Gorer, *The Life and Ideas of the Marquis de Sade*, (London: P. Owen, 1953), 223.
29. *Story of O*, 78–79.

8

Charles Sanders Peirce and Love as Evolutionary Principle

Mechanism has spawned many philosophical reactions to it, from romanticism to Dadaism to surrealism to dialogical thinking to existentialism to deconstructionism, and in each one we may find love's presence. I have suggested in the last chapter that the mechanistic metaphysics that has been so pivotal in shaping the modern soul, the modern vocabulary and its institutions, including that most ubiquitous of social forms, the modern secular nation-state,—a hybrid of Enlightenment reason and faith, and romantic sentiment,—is a metaphysics that dissolved love into pleasure.

I have decided to conclude with an analysis of a little-known essay by the great American pragmatist, Charles Sanders Peirce. The reason I do so is because he makes an argument which puts love within the cosmos, and thus resists the temptation to remain with the enlightenment's elevation of the self to a sovereign. Further, while Sade enabled us to see love in the context of modern metaphysics by having us approach it through pleasure that turns out to be nothing but evil itself, Peirce refuses to allow that the thought template which is so essential for the worlds we moderns are building is loveless. That the new world would be so loveless was Pascal's great fear, and it was behind his animosity to Descartes who would eclipse the living love of God by the innate idea of a perfect being who, ultimately, has no relationship to us. The Kantian shelter of the free self for all its philosophical cleverness asks us to accept a mere possibility. But if one thinks that love is essential to nourishing us and giving us a self that might not be autonomous but is more capable of contributing more to a better world than being moral and reasonable (whatever those terms may mean), one is unlikely to be happy dwelling in the thought of one's own dignity. Whether Peirce is right or not is, in my view, less interesting than his insight that love evolves and that its evolution takes place within life, that it too is part of the universe.

Peirce is probably America's greatest philosopher of the nineteenth and earliest twentieth century. He was a great logician, metaphysician, and he remains a towering figure in the field of semiotics. Peirce held, as I do, that the truth of something and its meaning are bound up with the effects that it generates.[1] As a semiotician he takes signs seriously, and this enables him to consider theology seriously, for theology is not primarily about objects, but about signs, and signs tell us all manner of things about a people and its time, including its emotional and linguistic worlds which are certainly real for them. At a time when Darwin's theory of evolution had largely completed the mechanistic paradigm by uprooting purpose from its last hiding place in nature, in complex organic forms, Peirce proposed a theory of "Evolutionary Love" in his *Scientific Metaphysics*. Peirce's work is an intriguing admixture of metaphysics of science and theology: his argument, while attentive to the fundamental breakthrough that had been made in our study of nature and, in keeping with his whole demeanor, steeped in an "objectivist" spirit, which kept him a soldier of the spirit of science, never takes its eye off what he sees as the real framing or metaphysics of nature. Nor does he disregard the human world and the ideas it has generated about the sources of life's powers. In other words, he does not commit the nonanthropomorphic fallacy of Descartes and Spinoza of taking himself out of nature as he explores it.

According to Peirce there are three alternative evolutionary principles, what he calls the tychastic (evolution by fortuitous variation), the anancastic (evolution by mechanical necessity), and the agapastic (creative love). All three principles, he claims, "are composed of the same general elements," but "agapism exhibits them the most clearly."[2] Peirce contrasts the rule of love, which he formulates thus "sacrifice your own perfection to the perfection of your neighbor" (191) with the utilitarian doctrine which speaks of the greatest good of the greatest number. The distinctive feature of the commandment of love is the requirement that love is directed to persons not abstractions—not to people we do not know but those in the purview of our life and feeling.

The first evolutionary principle considered by Peirce, evolution via mechanical principles, is refuted on the following grounds:

> First, because the principle of evolution requires no extraneous cause, since the tendency to growth can be supposed itself to have grown from an infinitesimal germ accidentally started. Second, because law ought more than anything else to be supposed a result of evolution. Third, because exact law obviously can never produce heterogeneity out of homogeneity; and arbitrary heterogeneity is the feature of the universe of the most manifest and characteristic. Fourth, because the law of the conservation of energy is equivalent to the proposition that all operations governed by mechanical laws are reversible; so that an immediate corollary from it is that growth is not explicable by those laws, even if they be not violated in the process of growth.[3]

The astuteness of Peirce's refutation rests upon the problem of origin and tracing origin back to the farthest point. The modern revivalists of mechanism had all sought to make the laws of the universe there right at the start. Three primary explanations were given: God started the world (Descartes), the world is God (Spinoza), and the mind makes law and we have no legitimate right to conceive of a time before the world (Kant). In each case we have a view of the universe that antecedes the principle of evolution, though Peirce alerts us to the more significant point that a mechanistic explanation stands in fundamental tension with it.

Let us consider these three possibilities a little more closely. In the case of Descartes, God serves a useful explanatory purpose, but it is essentially not only a metaphysical origin but a theological one. Although the ego and then God are used to lay foundations for a way of seeing the universe as governed by law, the origin itself is not subject to the law at the beginning of creation. Only after creation is God not entitled to perform miracles. The reason Descartes gives for God not interfering in nature in a manner contrary to mechanical law is that God is not a deceiver. Again, we have a nonscientific grounding which is meant to ensure the prospects of science. Descartes's position, then, is not scientific, but speculative. Insofar as he makes God's will constrained by a mind that is accessible to the human understanding, he has remained anchored in a theological tradition going back to the Greeks. (See Plato's *Euthyphro* where the point is made that the god loves the holy/pious because it is holy/pious, and the holy is not simply a product of the God's caprice.) Just as there is no scientific reason for accepting the hypothesis of God as creating the universe, even if one were to accept the Aristotelian argument of a first cause, a prime mover, there is no necessary theological one of assuming that God created the universe as subject to mechanical laws from the start. Peirce's point is not that mechanical explanations are ipso facto untrue, only that evolution is not explained by mechanism, and hence that mechanism is a later emergent. Historically we know that our knowledge of those laws is a late product of the evolution of consciousness.

In the case of Spinoza, we see the Stoic roots of the doctrine. Spinoza leaves the question unasked, while the Stoics held (as, of course, did the Spinozian Nietzsche) that the universe did not start out of a single event, but that it endlessly repeated itself. This may be much more satisfying to our speculative imagination, but it too is not a result of science but of speculation or logical inference of the (as yet) undemonstrable. The speculation is only tenable to the extent that it does not violate the most reasonable scientific hypothesis. That hypothesis must sustain the idea that the universe is not in infinite drift and that there was no origin. At present, cosmologists favor the very hypothesis which refutes the cosmos as an endless cycle of explosions and contractions. The problem still remains for Spinoza that if the universe evolves out of an "infinitesimal germ accidentally started" the sturdiness of the mechanism falters.

Kant's explanation avoided both these pitfalls. He needed neither theology to explain the origin of the universe nor a Stoic cosmology which might be refuted. His weakness was that some of the conditions which he identified as the essential conditions of mechanism (in particular the necessity of Euclidean space and a universe in which objects were strictly reciprocal, causally related, and parts of a continuum) have come into question with the modern consensus of physicists, which, respectively, calls for non-Euclidean theories of space and which disrupts the implacability of the continuum (quantum mechanics). Even apart from that, Kant is still loaded with the essential problem that an accidental beginning is prohibited from the outset. In Kant, all talk of beginning is off-limits because time is the condition of a possible experience, so to talk about what is itself the empirical condition of time is forbidden. While Kant's theory of the subjectivity of time is not a silly piece of relativism and a genuine attempt to mediate between the conundrums of absolute framing and relative position, the theory breaks down under the inadequacy of its logical, mathematical, and cognitive building blocks.

In all three evolutionary principles examined by Peirce, there is an unshakable faith in the universe being law-governed. There is also the need to resort to a metaphysical explanation is required because a scientific one cannot be found. Only Descartes resorts to a theological metaphysics, one which is, at the very least, highly contestable on theological grounds. When La Place said he had no need of the hypothesis of God, he was, in effect, asking us to give up all such metaphysical speculation because it was not necessary. And from the perspective of everyday science he was right. However, as we have seen above there was not only no necessary discontinuity between mechanism and a concept of a supreme being which created the world, but metaphysicians felt compelled in some way to bring that sign into their system, even as world or mere idea. La Place's boldness was ultimately based upon indifference to metaphysical completeness. The best that we can do regarding the principle of mechanical causation, once Kantianism can no longer be defended as certain, is to say that certain types of phenomena conform to the principle. Peirce goes a step further saying that:

> in regard to...exactitude, all observation is directly opposed to it [i.e., the exactness and universality of regularity in nature]; and the most that can be said is that a good deal of this observation can be explained away. Try to verify any law of nature and you will find that the more precise your observations, the more certain they will be to show irregular departure from the law. We are accustomed to ascribe these, and I do not say wrongly, to errors of observation; yet we cannot usually account for such errors in any antecedently probable way. Trace their cause back far enough and you will be forced to admit they are always due to arbitrary determinations or chance.[4]

Generally the question of the evolutionary character of the universe has only served to highlight the derivative character of mechanism. This in no way limits what can be observed as conforming to mechanical patterns, but it should put a stop to claims that everything that is can and must be explained in terms of these patterns. Peirce's point about the patent predominance of heterogeneity within our universe serves to reinforce this conclusion.

Peirce's critique of fortuitous variation or chance is similar to his critique of mechanism in that he does not wish to refute the fact that a wide array of phenomena can be observed as falling under this evolutionary principle. His point is not that we might not be able to observe the mutation of species and evolving complexity, but that chance alone does not account for all of what evolves.

As Peirce realized in his day, the idea of evolution by chance has become the dominant one. The metaphysical implication of evolution by chance (one slowly drawn by Darwin himself) is that God is not needed. Like mechanism, though, the cosmology can only deal with phenomena and nothing in and of itself discounts the possibility of a power that sets this world in motion. But there is no necessary reason for introducing a principle alien to the theory itself other than a sense of intellectual or moral discomfort in making chance alone the basis of life. The sense of discomfort which has always been felt by critics of the idea of chance as the source of order is the chasm between an origin of absolute contingency and simplicity, and a pattern of complexity and order. Just as the critic of the mechanistic principle points to the vastness of irregularity in the universe, the critic of tychastic evolution will point to the vastness of regularity. Peirce himself is sympathetic to the emphasis upon contingency and spontaneity that is so fundamental to tychastic evolution. But he sees a couple of problems which, when taken together, suggest that what he finds unacceptable is the idea of positive evolutionary consequences emerging from strife and selfishness[5]:

> [I]n the tychastic evolution progress is solely owing to the distribution of the napkin-hidden talent of the rejected servant among those not rejected, just as ruined gamesters leave their money on the table to make those not yet ruined so much the richer. It makes the felicity of the lambs just like the damnation of the goats, transcribed to the other side of the equation.[6]

If this argument were to be taken on its own, I could not agree with Peirce. It seems to me that a huge evolutionary advance was made when the classical tenet of "like produces like" was dispensed with and the alchemical traditions' emphasis upon transmutation of the base into the higher was widely adopted in the sphere of politics, economics, and industry. It was not that selfishness was suddenly introduced into the world, as if its presence was not discernible in every tyrant and gang of bandits, but that the expansion of units taken as selves had the effect of counterbalancing the effects of a few selves constraining the self-development of other selves. All the time, though, other socializing forces were at play, not least a religious-moral code emphasizing the well-being of the neighbor, to mitigate (albeit frequently without success) the more deleterious effects of selfishness. In England, for example, the rapidity of the development of a social variety of liberalism in the nineteenth and well into the twentieth century was widely accepted, even among the Conservative Party, as the inevitable accompaniment of a market society.

Peirce's sharp words about modern economics reinforce his opposition to the alchemical character of modernity. My position concurs with Peirce's on the different plane of the general argument about the superiority of an agapastic principle. That is, the egocentrism of market societies I think does account for part of their success, but there is a point at which such egocentrism threatens to undermine the very prospect of there being rules at all. In part, this is when the rules that frame the market simply shroud utterly false or nonsubstantial economic transactions (the various forms of pyramid schemes which lead to financial crashes) and/or the dangerously high level of litigation that takes place in market societies rip apart the social fabric. In this respect, some of the alchemical triumphs which characterize modernity are also corrosive of the spiritual well-being of its neighbors. It is in this sense that I agree with Peirce.

But there is another of Peirce's arguments that is very important in his elevation of love above chance as the primary evolutionist principle, and that is the capacity of mind to integrate ideas and to become (potentially) increasingly purposeful about our world, including our past and future. According to Peirce a tychastic evolutionary model will indeed account for contingencies of social existence, but not for the purposeful pattern that is discernible by people when they speak of a common "spirit" of an age, people, or culture. Peirce does not mention this, but I think it is quite astonishing how a theory based on mechanical chance tends to smuggle in a metaphysics of purposefulness without even a blink. Thus, in discussions of behavior which are governed by a tychastic model of evolution the individual is spoken of as if s/he is acting for the good of the species and in one and the same breath it becomes (seemingly) reasonable to be antialtruistic and altruistic, to act solely for one's own apparent well-being and the well-being of the species. Peirce thinks that the confluence of shared purposes is itself indicative of a principle other than mere chance at work, and that confluence is due to a patterning that comes from mind itself evolving as well as the world within which it operates. The integration and continuity that occurs in the historical consciousness is not

145

then simply a chance product but a characteristic of mind itself. It is important, Peirce himself realized, not to confuse this with a Hegelian model of history. For Hegel, the chance element is too downplayed and history takes on too much of a legal straightjacket, a demand that places the philosopher in the position of having to explain and defend the straitjacket.

Both evolution through necessity and evolution through chance are one-sided principles which become reconciled through the agapastic principle. For Peirce, then, it is not that necessity or chance are not part of the process; the point is that they both are and that something else needs to be introduced to account for them. According to Peirce:

> All three modes of evolution are composed of the same general elements. Agapism exhibits them the most clearly. The good result is here brought to pass, first, by bestowal of spontaneous energy by parent upon the offspring, and second by the disposition of the latter to catch the general idea of those about it and thus to serve the general purpose.[7]

Love is the integrative principle which requires increasing integration of parts and a communication between parts. Note too that Peirce conceives of mind as extending beyond consciousness. Thus, feeling, for example, is for Peirce a mental experience, but our consciousness of it is not precise in the way that it might be of an idea. Love, then, in Peirce's sense is deployed as a principle to explain shared sympathies and collective enterprises even though the enterprises may not be articulated in conscious terms. According to Peirce:

> The agapastic development of thought is the adoption of certain mental tendencies, not altogether heedlessly, as in tychasm, nor quite blindly, as in anacasm, but by an immediate attraction for the idea itself, whose nature is divined before the mind possesses it, by the power of sympathy, that is by virtue of the continuity of mind; and this mental tendency may be of three varieties, as follows. First, it may affect a whole people or community in its collective personality, and be thence communicated to such individuals as are in powerfully sympathetic connection with the collective people, although they may be intellectually incapable of attaining the idea by their private understandings or even perhaps of consciously apprehending it. Secondly, it may affect a private person directly, yet so that he is only enabled to apprehend the idea, or to appreciate its attractiveness, by virtue of his sympathy with his neighbors, under the influence of a striking experience or development of thought.... Third,

it may affect an individual, independently of his human affections by virtue of an attraction it exercises upon his mind, even before he has comprehended it.[8]

If love is the evolutionary principle, then one may reply: well why is there so much violence in the world? And is it really any less than before? The reply to this is that the violence is the impediment of the principle and that there is the opportunity for a growing awareness of its causes and the need to overcome it. Love works slowly and each catastrophe is the demonstration of love's failure to achieve its supremacy. Moreover, Love is not the only power in life, even if it is the one that resolves the collision of contingencies. The slow accretion of a historical memory of lack of love (including injustice) is part of the evolutionary process itself. Note central to this reasoning is the all-important point of putting all of what human beings do firmly back into the cosmos and not treating our relationships as anomalies within the cosmos. The bias of making social life conform to a discourse observing mere forces has long since lost any legitimacy. One does not even have to claim that love underpins all of creation to affirm that for human beings it is the supreme evolutionary principle. That the principle naturally requires that it be extended beyond love of each other and to all creatures and ultimately to life itself may well be one reason why Christianity itself had to become increasingly ecumenical, had to move beyond itself, opening itself to other religions and evolve secular formations based upon tolerance and mutual respect.

As positive as Peirce is about Christianity as an evolutionary force, he also puts his finger on a deficiency that is embedded in the New Testament and hence can be said to be carried through Christianity from the time of the compilation of the canonical texts of the New Testament. That is its tendency, which he believed was particularly conspicuous in the *Book of Revelation*, to make justice override love—a tendency that I think is perennial and indicative of the slowness of love's labor and the hunger for an immediate "solution" to human suffering.[9] Peirce is not without compassion for the early Christians whose patience, he believes, was worn down by the greed and heartlessness of Rome, but for him it is impossible to ignore the bitterness and vengefulness that pervade the *Book of Revelation*. For Peirce, the great Christian truth was that "God sent not the Son into the world to judge the world; but that the world should through him be saved. He that believeth on him is not judged: he that believeth not hath been

A Philosophical History of Love

judged already.... And this is the judgment, that the light is come into the world, and that men love darkness rather than the light."[10]

Peirce's answer to the existence of hatred and evil in a universe created out of and evolving by, through, and into love is to take darkness as "merely the defect of light, so hatred and evil are mere imperfect stages of love and loveliness."[11] Punishment in this case becomes the experience that comes with the choice of the "defective."[12] The personification of evil, the devil, then, is not a coordinate power but a subordinate which must be drawn into it: "the love that God is, is a love which embraces hatred as an imperfect stage of it, an Anteros (yea even needs hatred and hatefulness) as its object."

The very possibility of a God that is the name given to the source of cosmic love, and the belief that love is the supreme power behind creation, militates against revenge or even justice being the primary purpose of creation. Divine justice is divine because it is secondary to divine love. To believe in eternal damnation or annihilation is to believe that either God is impatient, makes mistakes, or is frustrated by time. It is not suffering or punishment per se that is ruled out of possibility: the only punishment that can rightly be called divine punishment is a divine way of bringing one into momentary alignment in order to make one open to love by enhancing one's understanding of what one has done.

That love is not defeated by the hatred of evil is put beautifully by Peirce when he writes: "Love, recognizing germs of loveliness in the hateful, gradually warms it into life, and makes it lovely."[13]

But what of all this talk of God? Surely there is no need for such talk anymore. I have used the term because Peirce found himself resorting to one of metaphysics' oldest signs. Some insist we must not use it anymore. But love is stronger than the signs we use to express it. And yet—must we not sign?

Notes

1. See my opening to *Power, Love and Evil*.
2. Charles Sanders Peirce, *Scientific Metaphysics Volume VI, Collected Papers of Charles Sanders Peirce*, ed. Charles Hartshorne and Paul Weiss (Cambridge, MA: Harvard University Press, 1935), 203.
3. Ibid., 16.
4. Ibid., 37.
5. Peirce's critique of tychastic evolution does not seem to me satisfactorily developed in any one place in *Scientific Metaphysics* and ultimately rests upon his view of the universe as essentially mindful. But this is simply to

emphasize that as we are creatures of meaning—enmeshed in signs—we
have no right to see that this is not a quality of the universe itself.

6.   Ibid., 203–4.
7.   Ibid., 203.
8.   Ibid., 205–6.
9.   But for a fascinating reading of Revelation which is both sophisticated and
     completely at odds with Peirce's statements see Jacques Ellul, *Apocalypse:
     The Book of Revelation*, trans. George Schreiner (New York: Seabury,
     1977).
10. Ibid., 208.
11. Ibid., 190. The choice of loveliness as a translation for αγαθον is an
     interesting one. The more accurate translation would be "good."
12. Ibid., 191.
13. Ibid., 192.

Conclusion

Peirce is a great philosopher and his reflections on love demonstrate that even the naturalistic scientific horizon could, for him at least, not shut love out as a cosmic principle. Peirce speaks as a philosopher and scientist who has been attuned to his Christian heritage. His appeal to love as a cosmic principle is done in the context of a view of life where modern science purportedly holds the key to the nature of nature. Of course, the modern scientific view of life has its origins in the Greek imagination which was able to dissolve the world into number (Pythagoras) and infinitely small particles, even though the moderns developed a more refined experimental model and the dynamism of infinitesimal calculus. But the troubling thing about making the world conform to the matrices of modern science was that its matrices reduce the world, and its triumphs in reduction are those less infused with spirit, whose actual characteristics are most capable of yielding what science wants to extract through its mathematical and experimental procedures. By contrast the human sciences have no such master method. For this reason while we can launch rockets into far away galaxies, we cannot stop gangs fighting, let alone help neighbors find peace in troubled spots like the Middle East.

Peirce was a man of the nineteenth century, and while his semiotics points the way to a view of the lifeworld far closer in spirit to the kinds of orientation made possible by phenomenologists and speech thinkers, his problem and his tools display an unshakeable faith in science. One might say that the overwhelming difference between the nineteenth and twentieth centuries was the widespread breakout of opposition in the human sciences to any attempt for a unified scientific theory which would enfold the babbling and singing lifeworld within the silent planes and vectors of nature as conceived by physics.

Many spirits vied for adoration within the twentieth century—the spirit of nationalism, the spirit of communism, the spirit of art, the spirit of science, and the spirit of commerce. And while humanity never serves just one spirit, tumult is assured when the spiritual powers vying for command pull peoples in contrary directions. If the outer history of the twentieth century is explosive, the interior history is implosive. Psychotherapy is the twentieth century's specialty for dealing with the interior disintegration that afflicts so many lives. Freud's great legacy consists in generating a practice that enables people to speak of their traumas and attempts to find themselves back to love. The proliferation of different types of therapy does not conceal the fact that so many of them seek to heal a broken self so that it may be more loving and more receptive to love. Therapy is a response to the isolation of the modern self and the need for that isolated self to express who it really is to somebody who will really hear them—for a fee. The fee is necessary for the presence of the analyst, who like just about everyone else is woven into the commercialized relationships of modern life. The Reformation's catch cry of "everyman a priest" did indeed help bring people into their respective stations where each could profess his calling through his service in the world (his profession), but the modern therapist is proof of the enduring need of continuance of a mediator between the one needing to see love's way and the seer of that way. We are a long way from the day "every person is a therapist."

Through Freud and Jung therapy has shown that it seeks to heal its patients by reference to narratives and archetypes of past peoples. Freud's excavation of the Greeks and his imaginings about tribes is no less vital to his legacy than his observations of Anna O, the rat man, the wolf man; likewise Jung's fascination with astrology, alchemy, the I-Ching, and Eastern religion. No less relevant is the widespread deployment among therapists of quasi-shamanic techniques. One of the great values of writings in the psycho-therapeutic tradition is its reactivation of the relevance of lost traditions. The rootlessness of the moderns is the curse that has accompanied their liberties. The liberty to be a sovereign self is the liberty to have an empire of inner nothingness—of course, not all are condemned to this nothingness, but the extent of those who experience freedom as vacuity is vast enough that it is a major concern. Thus, does the modern self seeks a spiritual content from somewhere—and the past which provides the archetypes of the therapeutic imagination was erected by bonds and codes of stringency which certainly formed definite selves—even the enslaved self was sure enough of his or her status and role and place, however miserable it was. It is along similar lines that the modern finds him or herself likely to be enchanted by the indigenous myths and lifeways which, however, materially impoverished, and socially despairing, still carry shards of enchantment which the modern European or Westerner longs to partake of, no matter how removed from his or her own roots. Psychotherapy thus provides a way in which present disintegration can find sustenance through being open to a process of integration that has proven itself over the Ages. To this considerable extent it may be of enormous benefit in enabling people to find some sense of wholeness in the modern world. And, to repeat, Freud's importance in this, irrespective of the specific form of therapy, lies in his elevation of speech to a healing role within a framework where speech has otherwise largely been deemed to be an irrelevance. Thus, Freud was able to reinsert the human qua human—the speaking animal as Aristotle rightly said, which is to say the animal who forms a future and resuscitates a past in a present through the power of significa-tion and communion. Speech is the bodybuilding process of human kind—and it is truly pitiful to hear people speak about language as if it were primarily a process of description of the world's flow that ever fails to succeed, as if names kill things. What are all human associa-tions, and all the external testaments of those associations—whether palaces, roads, bridges, libraries, courts, schools, playing fields, and battle fields—but testaments to authority and cooperation that were all activated via speech? Speech is only secondarily a descriptive power—it is primarily a creative and redemptive power. The speech or dialogi-cal thinkers from Feuerbach—who first stated that a community is an I-Thou relationship—to Rosenstock-Huessy, Rosenzweig, Buber, Ebner, and in Russia, quite independently, Bakhtin, all emphasize the creativity and fecundity, and redemptive power—the resuscitation of things spent and left dead—that comes through our power to respond to and call upon each other to make and review and remake ourselves, our world, our past, and our future. Description itself is, to borrow a Hegelian term, but a "moment" in the process of communion. Thus is our history also primarily a matter of speech. Speech so conceived is not the verbal as opposed to the written—that duality of form is like-wise of secondary importance—but of living expression which finds itself involved in future formation, and draws upon past and present as well as response to the compulsion to live further and more into the future as opposed to what is but the emission of stale and dead signs, i.e., the nonsignificant, the unredeemable.

Thus, the psychotherapist's gift is but itself the continuation of the gift of the sign, and the conveyance of the sign of love to those distracted, disturbed, traumatized, and lost souls whose experience of lovelessness and search for love brings them to the therapist. Love is energy and that is what the soul craves for in its continuance in creation, in its immortalizing; its reverse is evil, the decreation of hate, love in plummet, violent contagion, no less an energy, but one which would swallow up all future—exactly as Sade had expressed it—destroying the entire universe, if it had the capacity. Both spread through mimesis. The question is not that of being a sovereign self, as if a child could grow who did not copy his parents, siblings, fellows! It is imitating the right way to love, finding the right way to health of the soul. Therapy insofar as it has any value is the enabling of people to imitate what is lovable—lovable by God and lovable by those who seek life in its exuberance, which ultimately lies in the formation of convivial dwelling places, social bodies, whether with a family, with friends, or simply with neighbors and/or strangers who share common loves and needs.

We are task pursuers—even if rest and contemplation and quiet may provide anchorage or even meaning for our lives, even the most fundamental need such as the provision of bodily fuel for continuance will pull upon the person as a task. Tasks are all around us, whether chosen or enforced. We all require integration with another body in order to pursue our tasks and thus in order to find the energy either to persist or find fulfillment. The question is what capacities the body to which we attach ourselves has. All social bodies are potentially love's bodies. This is Freud, as much as Giordano Bruno, as much as Augustine. The difference between the bodies is the task and the kind of love.

Whatever truth there is in the Jewish Bible and the New Testament exists because it participates in the spirit of love; that love infuses the word but it is the love that creates the next word, that cannot be contained in one institution or one book. But is this not the real meaning of the trinity, of the unity of Father, Son, and Spirit whose creations and tasks are never at rest in this life—which to be sure is a formulation anathema to the Jewish faith, but although differently formulated, is it not an insight retained from it? God is the name that is given to the place where love is created. And wherever there is creation, there is the potential for love to be found. That is ultimately also why there is no tradition which at some point does not find itself confronted by what is the greatest of all powers, and, simultaneously, no tradition which has not found its love confronted by the demonic wearing all its trappings.

The only God that is real is the one whose manifestations of love are inescapable. Everything else is superstition, words. The men who stone adulterers, the people who persecute another simply because of who they are, or because their transgression taps into their fear of life, of love—they can name their God whatever they want, but it is still the God of hatred and fear, the God of evil they worship and whose coming they celebrate and witness. That God wants victims to be thrown to it. The God of love, on the other hand, simply wants to do His work, which is to love. That work, that love, is far more important than submission to an emphatic insistence upon the signs by which it is designated. Love changes the signs through which it enters into and recreates the world, just as it moves about ever seeking its own expansion, returning again to the world in different guises to open a way out of the various hells we go into when we fail to follow its lead.

Index